Also in This Series

Family Favorite Casserole Recipes:
103 Comforting Breakfast Casseroles, Dinner Ideas,
and Desserts Everyone Will Love

No-Bake Desserts:
103 Easy Recipes for No-Bake Cookies, Bars, and Treats

Everyday Dinner Ideas:
103 Easy Recipes for Chicken, Pasta, and
Other Dishes Everyone Will Love

Easy Cookie Recipes:
103 Best Recipes for Chocolate Chip Cookies, Cake Mix Creations,
Bars, and Holiday Treats Everyone Will Love

Essential Slow Cooker Recipes:
103 Fuss-Free Slow Cooker Meals Everyone Will Love

Retro Recipes from the '50s and '60s:
103 Vintage Appetizers, Dinners, and Drinks Everyone Will Love

Homemade Soup Recipes:
103 Easy Recipes for Soups, Stews, Chilis, and Chowders Everyone Will Love

Easy Chicken
Recipes

Easy Chicken Recipes

103 Inventive Soups, Salads, Casseroles, and Dinners Everyone Will Love

Addie Gundry

St. Martin's Griffin ☙ New York

EASY CHICKEN RECIPES. Text and photographs © 2018 by Prime Publishing, LLC. All rights reserved. Printed in the United States of America. For information, address St. Martin's Press, 175 Fifth Avenue, New York, N.Y. 10010.

www.stmartins.com

Photographs by Megan Von Schönhoff and Tom Krawczyk

The Library of Congress Cataloging-in-Publication Data is available upon request.

ISBN 978-1-250-14628-1 (paperback)
ISBN 978-1-250-14634-2 (ebook)

Our books may be purchased in bulk for promotional, educational, or business use. Please contact your local bookseller or the Macmillan Corporate and Premium Sales Department at 1-800-221-7945, extension 5442, or by email at MacmillanSpecialMarkets@macmillan.com.

First Edition: March 2018

10 9 8 7 6 5 4 3 2 1

To the thirteen who took me glamping.
There is no group more generous, more loving, and more fun
that I know. Thank you for embracing the wilderness and enduring
the bugs, lack of light, and furry friends at night.
When I think of chickens, I think of you all.

Contents

4
Slow Cooker

5
Skillet

6
Oven-Baked

7
Casseroles

Introduction

Chicken is one of those proteins that makes its way into your meals quite often, but somehow still gets slightly neglected. When I was growing up, there was always my favorite Chicken Noodle Soup (page 29) when I was feeling under the weather, and when I'm feeling festive, there's my husband's chicken barbecue (page 57), the one he boasts about every time he turns the grill on. With this book, you can indulge in Buffalo Chicken Sandwiches (page 50), and get a fresh start with Southwest Chicken Tortilla Pinwheels (page 14).

It took me a while to appreciate this particular poultry. I never considered chicken to be an indulgence, a fancy food, and I always thought of it as bland. That is, until recently. I went glamping with thirteen women in Prince Edward County, Canada. We spent four days camping, but the glamour of the location, tents, scenery, food, and wine made our trip worthy of the name "glamping." We dined on a big long table in the middle of a vineyard with chefs surrounding us, wine poured before our glasses reached empty, and chickens were not only celebrated on our plates but wandering around by our feet and held on our laps. If there was ever a farm-to-table moment, this was it. Our appreciation for the taste, the bounty that we were so fortunate to have, was omnipresent.

When I arrived home after this beautiful trip, I began to think of chicken as more of a recipe foundation to be celebrated. Chickens were, in fact, not bland, but a canvas ready for vibrancy. A surface that when tossed with lemon pepper (page 100), coated in cornflakes (page 17), or glazed with bourbon (page 5) was one of the most delicious flavors there could be. I recalled all the times when I made chicken in the past and realized how present it was in our lives. One of my favorite meals to make when entertaining is Chicken and Waffle Sliders (page 138), weeknights at home often consist of Weeknight Chicken Tacos (page 65), football on Sunday is accompanied by Oven-Baked Parmesan Chicken Wings (page 22), and when that first snow falls, there is White Chicken Chili (page 41) in the slow cooker. Chicken has always been, though formerly perhaps a bit unconsciously, one of my favorites.

Putting together this collection of recipes, I couldn't stop at 100. It felt so rigid, and so I made it to 103. Why 103? When you come to our house, we want you to know you can always bring a friend, or two, or three. There is always room for three more. I invite you to dive into the chapters, the recipes, and recall the many times you've used chicken to make a meal, or a memory.

—Addie Gundry

1

Appetizers

Nothing says game day, backyard barbecue, or
family time like a memorable chicken appetizer. From
wings to rolls, salads to potstickers, this chapter has all the
recipes you need to feed your friends and family.

Bourbon Chicken and Biscuits

Yield: Serves 6 | Prep Time: 10 minutes | Cook Time: 20 minutes

While this dish works well as a main course, you can also enjoy it as a group where you gather together a few friends, grab some pull-apart buttermilk biscuits to dip in the bourbon sauce, and slice up into small sandwiches. Enjoy this dinner on a cool fall night or as a brunch dish to share in the morning.

INGREDIENTS

2 tablespoons olive oil

4 boneless, skinless chicken breasts

1 (16-ounce) container cremini mushrooms, sliced

1 cup bourbon

1 cup maple syrup

1 cup heavy cream

3 sprigs fresh thyme

1 teaspoon kosher salt

1 teaspoon freshly ground black pepper

1 (16.3-ounce) can refrigerated original biscuits

DIRECTIONS

1. In a large saucepan, heat the olive oil over medium heat. Add the chicken. Sear on one side for 5 minutes. Flip over and add the mushrooms, bourbon, and maple syrup. Bring to a simmer and cook for 10 minutes.

2. Add the cream, thyme, salt, and pepper. Cook for another 5 minutes.

3. Bake the biscuits according to package instructions.

4. Serve warm.

Slow Cooker Buffalo Chicken Dip

Yield: Serves 6 | Prep Time: 5 minutes | Cook Time: 4 hours

During football season, I'm always hearing random bursts of shouting in the other room as the home team fumbles yet another play. Even when the game disappoints, I like to make sure the food doesn't, and this crowd-pleasing dip wins the living room over every time.

INGREDIENTS

3 boneless, skinless chicken breasts, cooked and shredded (about 3 cups)

2 cups shredded mozzarella cheese

1 cup bottled hot sauce

1 cup sour cream

1 (8-ounce) package cream cheese, softened

5 ounces crumbled blue cheese

2 tablespoons dry ranch salad dressing mix

Parsley, for garnish (optional)

Corn chips and celery sticks for dipping, reserving celery leaves, for garnish (optional)

DIRECTIONS

1. Spray the insert of a 6-quart slow cooker with cooking spray.

2. In the slow cooker, combine the shredded chicken breast, mozzarella cheese, hot sauce, sour cream, cream cheese, blue cheese, and dry ranch salad dressing mix and stir until well mixed. Cover, and cook for 4 hours on Low.

3. Garnish with parsley and celery leaves, if desired. Serve warm, with corn chips and celery sticks for dipping.

NOTES

To cook the chicken, place the breasts on a baking sheet and bake at 350°F for 30 minutes.

Chicken Egg Rolls

Yield: 12 egg rolls | Prep Time: 30–35 minutes | Cook Time: 12–18 minutes

"Girls' night in" calls for a glass of white wine and egg rolls over gossip and chatting about the latest TV shows. Prepping these together is a fun group activity to help you bond or break the ice. And here's a tip: I like to fry these with the seam side down first to help seal in the filling.

INGREDIENTS

½ cup soy sauce

¼ cup packed light brown sugar

1 tablespoon grated fresh ginger

3 garlic cloves, minced

6 cups shredded Chinese (napa) cabbage

1 large carrot, grated

3 green onions, chopped

1 boneless, skinless chicken breast, cooked and diced (about 1 cup)

12 egg roll wrappers

1 large egg, lightly beaten

Oil (canola, vegetable, or peanut), for frying

Sweet-and-sour and/or spicy mustard sauces, for dipping

DIRECTIONS

1. In a small bowl, combine the soy sauce, brown sugar, ginger, and garlic.

2. In a large bowl, combine the Chinese cabbage, carrot, green onions, and chicken. Pour the soy sauce mixture over the cabbage mixture and toss. Let it stand for 10 minutes.

3. Place the cabbage mixture in a colander and drain well, squeezing out the liquid.

4. Place about ½ cup of the cabbage mixture onto the center of one egg roll wrapper. Lightly brush the edges with beaten egg. Fold one corner over the mixture, then fold both sides over the top, then roll up tightly. Repeat with the remaining filling and wrappers.

5. In a deep, medium skillet, heat about 1½ inches of oil over medium heat until hot but not smoking.

6. Add the egg rolls in batches and fry for 3–4 minutes on each side until golden. Remove with tongs or a skimmer and drain on paper towels.

7. Serve the egg rolls warm with sweet-and-sour and/or spicy mustard dipping sauces.

NOTES

To cook the chicken, place the breast on a baking sheet and bake at 350°F for 30 minutes.

Chicken Cakes and Rémoulade Sauce

Yield: Serves 8 | Prep Time: 30 minutes plus 30 minutes chilling | Cook Time: 6–8 minutes

You don't have to wait for Mardi Gras to break out the rémoulade sauce! This New Orleans specialty is a fun side to whip up any time you're expecting company. Feel free to repurpose it to serve alongside shrimp or crab cakes.

INGREDIENTS

Chicken Cakes

4–5 tablespoons olive oil

¼ cup finely diced red bell pepper

¼ cup finely diced green bell pepper

¼ cup finely diced celery

2 garlic cloves, minced

½ teaspoon kosher salt

¼ teaspoon freshly ground black pepper

3 boneless, skinless chicken breasts, poached and chopped (about 3 cups) (see note)

⅓ cup mayonnaise

1 tablespoon fresh lemon juice

1 tablespoon chopped fresh flat-leaf parsley

1 teaspoon dry mustard

¼ teaspoon ground red pepper

1½ teaspoons Old Bay seasoning

1 teaspoon dried tarragon

2 cups panko bread crumbs

2 large eggs, beaten

Rémoulade Sauce

⅓ cup mayonnaise

¼ cup chili sauce

2 teaspoons fresh lemon juice

2 teaspoons minced green onion

1 teaspoon capers, chopped

½ teaspoon Old Bay seasoning

¼ teaspoon Worcestershire sauce

1 teaspoon Dijon mustard

1 teaspoon garlic powder

A few drops of hot sauce

DIRECTIONS

1. *For the chicken cakes:* In a small sauté pan, heat 2 tablespoons of the olive oil over medium heat. Add the red and green bell peppers and the celery. Sauté until tender, then add the garlic, salt, and black pepper.

2. In a medium bowl, combine the chopped chicken, mayonnaise, lemon juice, parsley, mustard, ground red pepper, Old Bay seasoning, tarragon, and 1 cup of the panko. Mix well. Mix in the cooked vegetables and the beaten eggs.

3. Pour the remaining panko into a separate shallow bowl.

4. Using a large ice cream scoop, form the chicken cakes and coat with the panko.

5. Flatten the cakes slightly and then place on a baking sheet. Chill for 30 minutes. While the cakes are chilling, prepare the rémoulade sauce.

6. *For the rémoulade sauce:* In a small bowl, combine the mayonnaise, chili sauce, lemon juice, green onion, capers, Old Bay seasoning, Worcestershire, mustard, garlic powder, and hot sauce. Mix well and chill.

7. Heat 2 tablespoons of the olive oil in a large sauté pan over medium-high heat. Cook the chicken cakes for 3–4 minutes on each side until golden brown, adding the remaining 1 tablespoon olive oil if the pan looks dry.

8. Serve with the rémoulade sauce.

To poach the chicken, place the breasts in a pot. Cover with water. Bring to a boil. As soon as the water boils, reduce the heat to low, cover the pot, and allow the chicken to poach until done, 10–14 minutes, temperature for the chicken should be about 165°F.

Chunky Chicken Salad Cups

Yield: Serves 12 | Prep Time: 15 minutes | Cook Time: 7–8 minutes

Wonton cups, made with those thin wrappers you usually use when making egg rolls, are a must-have anytime you're expecting guests. You can put just about any kind of salad or dessert in them, and you've got an instantly sophisticated snack that guests can carry around easily while mingling. Experiment with different deli salad recipes to mix things up!

INGREDIENTS

12 wonton wrappers

2 boneless, skinless chicken breasts, cooked and chopped (about 2 cups)

¼ cup mayonnaise

3 tablespoons Major Grey's or other mango chutney

¾ teaspoon curry powder

¼ cup currants or dried cranberries

1 teaspoon minced onion

Pinch of kosher salt

Pinch of freshly ground black pepper

DIRECTIONS

1. Preheat the oven to 350°F. Coat a 12-cup muffin pan with cooking spray.

2. Place a wonton wrapper into each muffin cup, forming it against the bottom and sides of the cup, and bake for 7–8 minutes, until lightly browned. Allow cups to cool.

3. In a medium bowl, combine the chicken, mayonnaise, chutney, curry powder, currants, onion, salt, and pepper. Mix well.

4. Fill the wonton cups with the chicken salad. Serve.

NOTES

To cook the chicken, place the breasts on a baking sheet and bake at 350°F for 30 minutes.

Southwest Chicken Tortilla Pinwheels

Yield: Serves 4 | Prep Time: 5 minutes | Chill Time: 2 hours

No summer barbecue is quite complete without a few pinwheels spinning around. The addictive filling is all wrapped up in a neat little package, so you don't have to worry about making a mess everywhere.

INGREDIENTS

1 (8-ounce) package cream cheese, softened

3 tablespoons sour cream

1 (10-ounce) can RoTel tomatoes, drained and chopped

½ teaspoon kosher salt

½ teaspoon freshly ground black pepper

1 cup shredded cheddar cheese

4 green onions, thinly sliced

1 (15-ounce) can black beans, drained and rinsed

1 (15.2-ounce) can corn, drained and rinsed

½ cup cooked bacon, crumbled

1 jalapeño, seeded and finely diced

2 boneless, skinless chicken breasts, cooked and shredded (about 2 cups)

4 large burrito-size flour tortillas or wraps in the flavor of your choice

Potato chips, for serving

DIRECTIONS

1. In a large bowl using an electric mixer, combine the cream cheese, sour cream, tomatoes, salt, and pepper. Use a spoon to stir in the cheddar, green onions, black beans, corn, bacon, jalapeño, and shredded chicken.

2. Divide the mixture among the tortillas, spreading it out evenly and leaving a border at the edge. Roll up tightly. Wrap the rollups snugly in plastic wrap and transfer to the refrigerator to chill for 2 hours or until ready to serve.

3. Remove from the refrigerator and slice crosswise into 2-inch pieces. Stick toothpicks in the center of each rollup, if you wish, to help keep it tightly rolled. Serve with potato chips alongside.

NOTES

To cook the chicken, place the breasts on a baking sheet and bake at 350°F for 30 minutes.

Honey Barbecue Chicken Poppers

Yield: Serves 4–6 | Prep Time: 20 minutes | Cook Time: 12–15 minutes

Do you always wimp out and order the mildest sauce with your wings? If you can't stand the heat, then these chicken poppers are going to be your new best friend. The sweet honey taste will allow even the faint of heart to join in on the chicken fun during game day.

INGREDIENTS

Chicken

2 pounds boneless, skinless chicken breasts, cut into bite-size pieces

1 cup all-purpose flour

4 cups cornflakes, crushed

½ teaspoon kosher salt

½ teaspoon freshly ground black pepper

½ teaspoon lemon seasoning

½ teaspoon garlic powder

½ teaspoon paprika

2 large eggs, lightly beaten

¼ cup whole milk

Honey Barbecue Sauce

1 cup barbecue sauce

¼ cup honey

¼ cup ketchup

DIRECTIONS

1. *For the chicken:* Preheat the oven to 400°F. Cover a baking sheet with aliminum foil.

2. Place the chicken in a large bowl and coat the pieces with the flour.

3. In a separate large bowl, combine the cornflakes, salt, pepper, lemon seasoning, garlic powder, and paprika.

4. Dip the chicken into the egg, a few pieces at a time, then roll the pieces in the cornflake mixture. Place on the prepared baking sheet. Repeat to coat all the chicken.

5. Bake for 12–15 minutes, until the chicken is cooked through.

6. *For the honey barbecue sauce:* In a large bowl, combine the barbecue sauce, honey, and ketchup.

7. Serve the chicken with the dipping sauce on the side.

Copycat Bang Bang Chicken

Yield: Serves 4 | Prep Time: 25–30 minutes | Cook Time: 12 minutes

Upon first glance, this recipe, inspired by one of my favorite Cheesecake Factory apps, may seem as if it has a lot of ingredients and steps, but the battered chicken and the dressing can all be done in advance.

INGREDIENTS

Chicken

1 cup buttermilk

1 large egg

¾ cup all-purpose flour

¼ cup cornstarch

2 tablespoons sriracha or other hot sauce

½ teaspoon curry powder

¼ teaspoon kosher salt

1 pound boneless, skinless chicken breasts or thighs, cut into 2-inch chunks

Dressing

½ cup mayonnaise

3 tablespoons sweet chili sauce

2 tablespoons honey

1–1½ tablespoons sriracha or other hot sauce

2–3 teaspoons fresh lime juice

1 teaspoon curry powder

Salad

1 (22-ounce) head romaine lettuce

½ cup salted dry roasted peanuts

½ cup unsweetened shredded coconut

2 tablespoons sesame seeds

3–4 green onions

1 small cucumber, thinly sliced

½ cup thinly sliced red bell pepper

For Frying

2 cups peanut or vegetable oil

2 cups panko bread crumbs

DIRECTIONS

1. *For the chicken:* In a large bowl, combine the buttermilk, egg, flour, cornstarch, sriracha, curry powder, and salt and mix well. Add the chicken pieces and set aside.

2. *For the dressing:* In a medium bowl, combine all the dressing ingredients. Set aside, or chill for up to 1 day.

3. *For the salad:* Chop the romaine into bite-size pieces, reserving 4 larger leaves for garnish.

4. In a dry skillet, separately toast the peanuts, coconut, and sesame seeds over medium heat until each is light golden brown and fragrant, 3–4 minutes. Place the chopped lettuce in the bottom of a large bowl and arrange whole leaves and cucumbers around the edge of the bowl.

5. *For frying:* In a deep skillet, heat the peanut oil to 350°F or until a piece of chicken bubbles furiously when dropped into the oil. Remove the chicken from the batter and toss it in the panko until well coated. Cook about half the chicken at a time in the hot oil, turning to brown all sides, for about 4 minutes. Drain on paper towels and repeat with the remaining chicken.

6. Trim the green onions, leaving some of the green tops on. Place the hot chicken pieces over the lettuce in the serving bowl and decorate the bowl with the cucumbers, green onions, and strips of red bell pepper. Serve with the dressing and sprinkle the peanuts, coconut, and sesame seeds on top; serve immediately.

Spicy Chicken Potstickers

Yield: 36 potstickers | Prep Time: 20–25 minutes | Cook Time: 10–15 minutes

These traditional Chinese dumplings are ideal when you're putting together a spread of appetizers as a munchable meal for guests. Who doesn't love snacking on bite-size food all evening? Don't forget to pick up some chopsticks at the grocery store for everyone to use!

INGREDIENTS

Potstickers

1 pound ground chicken

½ cup shredded cabbage

1 carrot, shredded

2 garlic cloves, minced

2 green onions, thinly sliced

1 tablespoon soy sauce

1 tablespoon hoisin sauce

1 tablespoon grated fresh ginger

2 teaspoons sesame oil

¼ teaspoon freshly ground white pepper

¼ teaspoon red pepper flakes

36 wonton wrappers

2 tablespoons vegetable oil

Chopped fresh parsley, for garnish

Dipping Sauce

½ cup soy sauce

½ cup rice vinegar

2 tablespoons honey

3 garlic cloves, minced

2 tablespoons minced fresh ginger

2 teaspoons toasted sesame seeds

2 teaspoons sesame oil

DIRECTIONS

1. *For the potstickers:* In a large bowl, combine the ground chicken, cabbage, carrot, garlic, green onions, soy sauce, hoisin sauce, ginger, sesame oil, white pepper, and red pepper flakes. Mix well.

2. To assemble the potstickers, place a wonton wrapper on a flat surface. Spoon 1 tablespoon of the filling into the center of the wrapper. Rub the edges of the wrapper with water. Fold the dough over the filling to create a half-moon, then pinch the edges to seal.

3. In a large skillet, heat the vegetable oil over medium heat. Add the potstickers in a single layer—do not crowd the pan. Cook until golden and crispy, 2–3 minutes per side.

4. Place the cooked potstickers on a wire rack set over a baking sheet while you finish cooking the remaining potstickers. Transfer to a serving platter and top with parsley.

5. *For the dipping sauce:* In a medium bowl, combine the soy sauce, vinegar, honey, garlic, ginger, sesame seeds, and sesame oil and whisk to mix.

6. Serve with the hot potstickers.

Oven-Baked Parmesan Chicken Wings

Yield: Serves 6–8 | Prep Time: 5 minutes | Cook Time: 45 minutes

It's so hard to please picky eaters sometimes. Everything needs to be cooked "just right" and can't have too many spices or garnishes. This recipe is so reliable because it's simple enough to keep even the most particular kids happy, yet flavorful enough to satisfy adult taste buds, too.

INGREDIENTS

24 chicken wings, separated

Kosher salt and freshly ground black pepper

¼ cup olive oil

½ cup (1 stick) unsalted butter

1 tablespoon chopped garlic

Zest and juice of 1 lemon

3 tablespoons chopped fresh parsley

¼ cup grated Parmesan cheese

Lemon wheels, for garnish

DIRECTIONS

1. Preheat the oven to 350°F. Cover a baking sheet with aluminum foil.

2. Place the chicken wings in a large bowl and toss with salt, pepper, and olive oil. Spread the wings in an even layer on the baking sheet. Bake for 20–25 minutes, until lightly golden.

3. Remove the baking sheet from the oven and carefully drain off any liquids. Heat the broiler to high. Broil for 15–20 minutes, until the wings are brown and crispy, flipping the wings carefully once about halfway through.

4. In a medium saucepan, melt the butter with the garlic over medium heat. Allow to heat together gently for 3–4 minutes, until just starting to brown. Add the lemon zest and juice. Pour the mixture into a large bowl. Add the parsley and season with salt.

5. Remove the crispy wings from the oven and transfer to the bowl with the butter mixture. Toss the wings to coat evenly. Transfer to a serving tray and sprinkle with the Parmesan. Garnish with lemon wheels and serve.

Thai Chicken Satay

Yield: 20 skewers | Prep Time: 30 minutes plus 1 hour marinade time | Cook Time: 30 minutes

This Thai restaurant specialty fits right in with your backyard spread. The skewers are easy to nibble on while chatting with friends and family, making these a summertime staple.

INGREDIENTS

Marinade

2 tablespoons fish sauce

2 tablespoons minced garlic

1 tablespoon soy sauce

1 tablespoon sugar

¼ teaspoon freshly ground black pepper

½ teaspoon ground turmeric

½ teaspoon ground coriander

¼ teaspoon cayenne pepper

1 tablespoon Massaman curry paste (see note)

½ cup coconut milk

2 pounds boneless, skinless chicken breasts, cut into 1-inch wide strips

Peanut Sauce

2 teaspoons Massaman curry paste

2 tablespoons fish sauce

Zest and juice of 1 lime

¼ cup creamy peanut butter

2 tablespoons sugar

1 teaspoon sriracha sauce, plus more as needed

2 cups coconut milk

½ cup crushed peanuts, plus more for garnish

DIRECTIONS

1. In a dish or pan, soak 20 wooden skewers in water for at least 3 hours to prevent burning.

2. *For the marinade:* In a large zip-top bag, combine all the marinade ingredients except the chicken and parsley. Squeeze the bag to mix well. Add the chicken pieces and seal the bag well. Squeeze the bag to coat the chicken with the marinade. Place the bag in the refrigerator for at least 1 hour.

3. *For the peanut sauce:* Meanwhile, in a medium saucepan, combine all the peanut sauce ingredients over medium heat. Cook, stirring continuously, until thickened slightly, 10–15 minutes. Garnish with additional crushed peanuts.

4. Preheat the broiler to high. Line a baking sheet with aluminum foil and top with a wire rack. Coat lightly with cooking spray.

5. Remove the marinated chicken from the bag. Skewer each piece lengthwise. Place on the rack, leaving space between each skewer.

6. Broil for 7–8 minutes, until lightly golden brown. Carefully flip each skewer and return to the oven. Broil on the second side for 5 minutes.

7. Transfer to a serving platter, garnish with parsley, and serve with the warm peanut sauce.

NOTES

You can find Massaman curry paste in the ethnic food aisle of most grocery stores. However, if you can't find it, feel free to substitute a mild curry powder mixed with a touch of five-spice powder.

2

Soups, Stews, Chilis, Chowders

With recipes like warm and cozy chicken noodle soup, hearty chicken chili, and creamy corn chowder, this chapter is filled with comforting traditions. Tex-Mex, tortellini, and wild rice add funky flavors and will make these new favorites.

Chicken Noodle Soup

Yield: Serves 6 | Prep Time: 15 minutes | Cook Time: 45 minutes

The only good thing about getting sick when you're a kid is getting a bowl of homemade chicken noodle soup. (Well, that and getting to watch Nickelodeon.) Any time you're feeling a little bit blue, a bowl of this from-scratch soup is sure to add some cozy comfort.

INGREDIENTS

1 tablespoon olive oil

2 boneless, skinless chicken breasts, chopped

½ large onion, diced

2 celery stalks, diced

2 carrots, sliced

½ cup white wine (optional)

2 garlic cloves, minced

Kosher salt and freshly ground black pepper

1 bay leaf

2 cups chicken broth, low-sodium preferred

6 ounces egg noodles

Lemon wheels, for garnish

Fresh parsley, for garnish

DIRECTIONS

1. In a large soup pot, heat the olive oil over medium heat. Add the chicken and cook until lightly golden brown on all sides, about 8 minutes. Add the onion, celery, and carrots. Cook until the vegetables are near tender and the onions are translucent, about 6 minutes. Add the white wine (if using) and reduce the heat to medium-low.

2. Add the garlic, salt, pepper, and bay leaf. Add the broth and 2 cups of water and bring to a boil. Reduce the heat to a simmer and cook, uncovered, for 20 minutes, or until the chicken is cooked through and the vegetables are fully tender.

3. Add the noodles and cook for an additional 7 minutes, until the noodles are al dente.

4. Remove from the heat and allow to cool slightly before serving. Garnish with lemon wheels and parsley.

Slow Cooker Tex-Mex Chicken Stew

Yield: Serves 8 | Prep Time: 5 minutes | Cook Time: 6 hours 15 minutes

You know it's fall when you break out the slow cooker. Let this cook while you're at work, or even better, let it cook on a weekend day while you're off picking apples or pumpkins, and come home to a bowl of stew to warm you right back up. Plus, it's fantastic in warm weather, too, because you don't have to turn the oven on!

INGREDIENTS

1½ cups diced onion

1 tablespoon minced garlic

1 tablespoon tomato paste

1½ teaspoons chili powder

1 teaspoon honey

1 (15-ounce) can diced tomatoes, undrained

1 (15-ounce) can chili beans, undrained

2 tablespoons pickled jalapeños, chopped

1 cup chicken broth, low-sodium preferred

1½ tablespoons all-purpose flour

1 tablespoon vegetable oil

2 pounds boneless, skinless chicken thighs

1 (11-ounce) can Mexican corn with bell peppers, drained

2 ounces cream cheese, softened

Sliced jalapeños, sliced green onions, and fresh parsley, for garnish

DIRECTIONS

1. Spray the insert of a 6-quart slow cooker with cooking spray.

2. Place the onion, garlic, tomato paste, chili powder, honey, canned tomatoes, beans, and jalapeños in the slow cooker. Add the broth and stir.

3. In a small bowl, stir the flour and vegetable oil together to make a smooth paste. Add to the slow cooker and stir. Place the chicken pieces over the top, pressing down to submerge them in the broth. Cover and cook for 6 hours on Low.

4. Remove the chicken pieces and shred or chop. Return the chicken to the slow cooker, add the corn, and set the slow cooker to High. In a small bowl, stir the cream cheese with a few tablespoons of the broth mixture until smooth, then stir this into the slow cooker. Cover and cook for 15 minutes. Serve garnished with jalapeños, green onions, and parsley.

Chicken and Dumplings

Yield: Serves 6 | Prep Time: 15 minutes | Cook Time: 45 minutes

Chicken and dumplings—it's one of those recipes that's passed down from generation to generation and always manages to hit the spot. I've added a shortcut here by using crescent roll dough, but feel free to substitute your favorite dumpling recipe.

INGREDIENTS

1 tablespoon olive oil

2 boneless, skinless chicken breasts, chopped

½ large onion, diced

2 celery stalks, diced

2 carrots, diced

2 garlic cloves, minced

Kosher salt and freshly ground black pepper

1 bay leaf

4 cups chicken broth, low-sodium preferred

1 cup frozen green beans

1 (8-ounce) can crescent roll dough

Chopped fresh parsley, for garnish

DIRECTIONS

1. In a large soup pot, heat the olive oil over medium heat. Add the chicken and cook until lightly golden brown on all sides, about 8 minutes. Add the onion, celery, and carrots. Cook until the vegetables are beginning to become tender and the onion is translucent, about 6 minutes.

2. Add the garlic, salt, pepper, and bay leaf. Add the broth and bring to a boil. Reduce the heat to a simmer and cook, uncovered, for 20 minutes, or until the chicken is cooked through and the vegetables are tender. Stir in the frozen green beans.

3. Open the crescent roll dough and cut each piece into quarters. Drop into the soup and cook for 10 minutes, until the dumplings are cooked through. Ladle into bowls, garnish with parsley, and serve.

Creamy Chicken and Mushroom Soup

Yield: Serves 6 | Prep Time: 10 minutes | Cook Time: 20 minutes

This thick, creamy soup is the kind you'll pack up in a thermos and take with you to work on a cold, blustery winter day.

INGREDIENTS

8 ounces boneless, skinless chicken thighs, cut into 1-inch pieces

1 teaspoon chopped fresh rosemary

½ teaspoon kosher salt, plus more as needed

¼ teaspoon freshly ground black pepper, plus more as needed

1 tablespoon olive oil

1 tablespoon unsalted butter

1 cup chopped green onions, including some of the tender green tops

¾ cup chopped celery, including some of the leafy greens

1 teaspoon minced garlic

1 teaspoon fresh thyme leaves, or ½ teaspoon dried thyme

1 small bay leaf

⅓ cup all-purpose flour

4 cups chicken broth, low-sodium preferred

1 cup half-and-half

Sprigs of fresh rosemary, for garnish

DIRECTIONS

1. In a small bowl, toss the chicken pieces with the rosemary, salt, and pepper. In a 6-quart heavy-bottom stockpot, heat the olive oil over medium-high heat. Add the chicken and sauté until lightly browned, stirring frequently, about 4 minutes. Remove the chicken from the pot with a slotted spoon and set aside.

2. In the same pot, add the butter, green onions, and celery and stir over medium-high heat until the onion is translucent, 3–5 minutes.

3. Add the garlic, thyme, and bay leaf and cook, stirring, for 1 minute more, until fragrant. Sprinkle the flour over the vegetables and cook, stirring, until the flour has been completely absorbed, about 1 minute.

4. Add the broth and whisk until the liquid thickens slightly. Return the chicken to the pot, reduce the heat to medium, and cook for 5 minutes. Taste and adjust the seasonings as necessary. Remove the bay leaf.

5. If desired, at this point remove 2 cups of the soup, including the solids, and blend in a blender or food processor until pureed, then return to the pot. This thickens the soup and gives it a nice texture.

6. Add the half-and-half and salt and pepper to taste and continue to heat over medium heat, stirring frequently, about 4 minutes, until heated through and the flavors have blended.

7. Serve garnished with sprigs of rosemary.

Slow Cooker Chicken and Tortellini Soup

Yield: Serves 10–12 | Prep Time: 10 minutes | Cook Time: 4 hours 15 minutes

Tortellini is already stuffed with a flavorful filling, so your dish is that much fancier without any extra effort. Feel free to experiment by subbing out the cheese-filled tortellini with chicken-filled tortellini, tricolored, or something new!

INGREDIENTS

1 cup finely diced celery

1 cup finely diced onion

1 cup finely diced carrot

2 tablespoons minced fresh parsley, plus more for garnish

2 tablespoons chopped fresh basil

1 large bay leaf

1 tablespoon minced garlic

Kosher salt

2 pounds boneless, skinless chicken breasts or thighs

6 cups chicken broth, low-sodium preferred

Freshly ground black pepper

12 ounces prepared cheese tortellini

DIRECTIONS

1. Spray the insert of a 6-quart slow cooker with cooking spray.

2. Place the celery, onion, carrot, parsley, basil, and the bay leaf in the slow cooker. On a work surface, mash the minced garlic and 1 teaspoon of the salt together to form a paste; sprinkle over the vegetables. Lay the chicken pieces on top and pour the broth over all. Cover and cook on Low for 4 hours.

3. Remove the chicken pieces and shred or chop. Return to the slow cooker. Taste and season with salt and pepper if necessary. Add the tortellini, cover, and cook for an additional 15–20 minutes, until softened. Remove the bay leaf and garnish with parsley. Serve.

Slow Cooker Chicken Wild Rice Soup

Yield: Serves 8–10 | Prep Time: 15 minutes | Cook Time: 3 hours on High or 6 hours on Low

This hearty whole-grain soup originated in Minnesota, where much of the wild rice sold in the United States is still grown and harvested entirely by hand. It will warm up a winter's evening in the best possible way. True wild rice is a dark brown seed harvested from rice paddies around the United States or in other countries. Since rice from different sources cooks at different speeds, watch for the grains to just begin to crack open and show the white interior, not completely split open and curl inside out.

INGREDIENTS

2 tablespoons unsalted butter

1 cup chopped red onion

1 cup sliced carrots

2 cups coarsely chopped button mushrooms

½ cup all-purpose flour

1 teaspoon kosher salt

½ teaspoon freshly ground black pepper

6 cups chicken broth, low-sodium preferred

8 ounces wild rice

1½ boneless, skinless chicken breasts, cooked and diced (about 1½ cups)

½ teaspoon dry thyme

Fresh parsely, for garnish

DIRECTIONS

1. In a large skillet, melt the butter over medium-high heat. Add the onion and carrots and sauté for 2 minutes. Add the mushrooms and cook, stirring frequently, until the mushroom liquid evaporates and they begin to brown around the edges. Sprinkle the flour, salt, and pepper into the pan and stir for 1 minute. Add 2 cups of the broth and stir until the sauce begins to bubble and thicken.

2. Spray the insert of a slow cooker with cooking spray. Transfer the mushroom mixture to a large slow cooker, add the wild rice, chicken, thyme, and the remaining 4 cups broth. Stir, cover, and cook for 6 hours on Low or for 3 hours on High. Taste and adjust the seasonings as necessary. Ladle into bowls, garnish with parsley, and serve.

NOTES

To cook the chicken, place the breasts on a baking sheet and bake at 350°F for 30 minutes.

White Chicken Chili

Yield: Serves 8 | Prep Time: 15 minutes | Cook Time: 50 minutes

Is there ever a bad time for a bowl of chili? It's the ultimate comfort food that truly shines in the fall or winter. All you need is a blanket and a dramatic movie, and you've got yourself the perfect night in.

INGREDIENTS

2 pounds boneless, skinless chicken breasts and thighs

4 cups chicken broth, low-sodium preferred

1 cup chopped onion

½ cup chopped celery

1 teaspoon minced garlic (optional)

2 teaspoons ground cumin

1 teaspoon kosher salt

½ teaspoon ground coriander

½ teaspoon dried oregano

1 cup corn kernels (frozen, fresh, or canned, drained)

1 (15-ounce) can navy or cannellini beans, drained

1 (4-ounce) can diced chiles, drained

1 cup sour cream, for garnish

1 lime, cut into wedges, for garnish

Sprigs of fresh cilantro, for garnish

DIRECTIONS

1. In a 6-quart heavy-bottom stockpot, combine the chicken, broth, onion, celery, and garlic (if using) over medium heat. Bring to a boil, then reduce the heat and simmer for 20 minutes. Remove the chicken from the pot and shred, placing the meat in a medium bowl. Sprinkle the chicken with cumin, salt, coriander, and oregano and toss well, then return the chicken and spices to the stockpot. Simmer for 20 minutes. Add the corn, beans, and chiles and simmer for 10 minutes. Taste and adjust the seasoning as necessary.

2. Serve in individual bowls garnished with sour cream, lime wedges, and cilantro.

Chicken and Corn Chowder

Yield: Serves 6–7 | Prep Time: 15 minutes | Cook Time: 30 minutes

Chowder is a mainstay in New England restaurants, and this Chicken and Corn Chowder shows you why! It's a made-from-scratch recipe, so you can add more or less of any ingredient to customize the dish to your taste. With a classic blend of potatoes, onion, corn, and chicken, you just know it's going to be worth the effort.

INGREDIENTS

4 tablespoons (½ stick) unsalted butter, diced

1 large red bell pepper, diced

1 onion, diced

4 garlic cloves, minced

⅓ cup all-purpose flour

5½ cups chicken broth, low-sodium preferred

½ cup white wine

3 Yukon Gold potatoes, peeled and cut into roughly ½-inch dice

1 tablespoon fresh thyme, minced

1 teaspoon kosher salt

½ teaspoon freshly ground black pepper

1 pound boneless, skinless chicken breasts, cooked and shredded

2½ cups fresh or frozen corn

1½ cups heavy cream

8 bacon slices, cooked and crumbled

Sprigs of fresh thyme, for garnish

DIRECTIONS

1. In a large pot, melt the butter. Add the bell pepper and onion and cook until tender, about 6 minutes.

2. Add the garlic and cook for 30 seconds.

3. Whisk in the flour and cook for 2 minutes, being careful not to burn the flour.

4. While whisking, add the broth and wine and whisk until blended.

5. Add the potatoes, thyme, salt, and black pepper.

6. Bring to a boil, then reduce the heat to medium-low and cook for 10 minutes, or until the potatoes are tender.

7. Add the chicken, corn, and cream. Simmer for 10–15 minutes, until heated through.

8. Ladle into bowls and serve topped with the crumbled bacon and thyme.

NOTES

To cook the chicken, place the breasts on a baking sheet and bake at 350°F for 30 minutes.

Slow Cooker Chicken and Vegetable Soup

Yield: Serves 4 | Prep Time: 15 minutes | Cook Time: 4 hours on High or 7 hours on Low

Veggies make any soup feel just a little bit healthier. This is a rainy day soup that fills you up after you've been splashing around in puddles or soaked from head to toe. Chock-full of summer veggies, all you need is one spoonful to help you unwind.

INGREDIENTS

1 pound boneless, skinless chicken breasts

1 carrot, diced

2 celery stalks, diced

1 small onion, diced

1 small zucchini, cubed

1½ cups fresh corn

1 (14-ounce) can fire-roasted diced tomatoes, undrained

2 garlic cloves, minced

1 teaspoon finely minced fresh thyme

2 teaspoons Worcestershire sauce

½ teaspoon kosher salt

½ teaspoon freshly ground black pepper

4 cups chicken broth, low-sodium preferred

Fresh basil, for garnish

DIRECTIONS

1. Spray the insert of a 6-quart slow cooker with cooking spray. Put the chicken breasts, carrot, celery, onion, zucchini, corn, tomatoes, garlic, thyme, Worcestershire sauce, salt, pepper, and broth in the slow cooker. Mix the ingredients together.

2. Cover and cook for 7 hours on Low or for 4 hours on High.

3. Remove the chicken from the slow cooker and shred, return to the slow cooker, and stir to incorporate.

4. Taste and season with salt and pepper, if needed. Ladle into bowls and serve, garnished with the basil.

NOTES

This soup can be prepared on the stovetop instead of in the slow cooker:

In a large pot, heat 1 tablespoon olive oil over medium heat. Add the carrot, celery, onion, and garlic and sauté for 4–5 minutes.

Add the zucchini and corn and cook for an additional 2–3 minutes. Add the tomatoes, garlic, thyme, Worcestershire sauce, salt, pepper, and broth. Stir to mix. Add the chicken to the pot and bring to a boil. Reduce to a simmer and cook until the chicken is tender and fully cooked, 1–1½ hours. Remove the chicken from the pot, shred, and return to the pot. Taste and season with salt and pepper, if needed.

3

Backyard Favorites

It's summertime. There's a light breeze in the air, soft music is playing, and you're setting up tables and chairs out back to celebrate anything from the Fourth of July to a nephew's graduation. The only thing missing is the perfect backyard spread. Bring out any of these chicken favorites, from the lettuce wraps to the tacos, for a real winner!

Southern-Style Chicken Salad

Yield: 4 cups | Prep Time: 10 minutes | Chill Time: 2 hours

Springtime is picnic time, as far as I'm concerned. I love breaking out the red checkered blanket and hiking up to one of my favorite benches close to my cabin in northern Minnesota. This chicken salad recipe is perfect to pack along for a well-earned sandwich after a long day of exploring.

INGREDIENTS

⅔ cup mayonnaise

3 tablespoons sweet pickle relish

1½ tablespoons Dijon mustard

1 teaspoon lemon pepper

½–1 teaspoon kosher salt

¼ teaspoon freshly ground black pepper

¼ teaspoon garlic powder

4 boneless, skinless chicken breasts, cooked and cut into bite-size pieces (about 4 cups)

1–2 celery stalks, finely chopped

2 green onions, finely chopped

1–2 hard-boiled eggs, chopped (optional)

Lettuce, bread, and/or crackers, for serving

DIRECTIONS

1. In a medium bowl, combine the mayonnaise, relish, mustard, lemon pepper, salt, black pepper, and garlic powder.

2. Mix in the chicken, celery, and green onions. Add hard-boiled eggs (if using). Mix again.

3. Cover and chill for 2 hours or longer.

4. Serve on a bed of lettuce with bread or crackers or in a sandwich.

NOTES

To cook the chicken, place the breasts on a baking sheet and bake at 350°F for 30 minutes.

Buffalo Chicken Sandwiches

Yield: Serves 6 | Prep Time: 15 minutes | Cook Time: 20 minutes

Add a little pep to your step! It can get really boring bringing a regular old peanut butter and jelly sandwich to work every day, which is why this buffalo chicken sandwich is just what you need. Pack it up and reheat before chowing down, and you'll be the envy of the office!

INGREDIENTS

⅔ cup hot pepper sauce

½ cup (1 stick) unsalted butter

1 tablespoon white vinegar

¼ teaspoon Worcestershire sauce

¼ teaspoon cayenne pepper

⅛ teaspoon garlic powder

¼ teaspoon kosher salt

4 boneless, skinless chicken breasts, cooked and shredded (about 4 cups)

6 buns, for serving

6 tablespoons ranch dressing

Thinly sliced mozzarella cheese and lettuce, for serving

DIRECTIONS

1. In a large pot, combine the hot pepper sauce, butter, vinegar, Worcestershire sauce, cayenne pepper, garlic powder, and salt. Bring to a simmer over medium heat while stirring with a whisk. As soon as the liquid begins to bubble on the sides of the pot, remove from the heat and continue to stir.

2. Add the chicken to the sauce.

3. Top each bun with 1 tablespoon of the ranch dressing, the lettuce, ⅔ cup of the chicken, and the mozzarella cheese, and serve.

NOTES

To cook the chicken, place the breasts on a baking sheet and bake at 350°F for 30 minutes.

Honey Mustard Chicken Avocado Bacon Salad

Yield: Serves 4 | Prep Time: 20 minutes plus 30 minutes marinade time | Cook Time: 8–10 minutes

Everything is better with some bacon and avocado, right? This may seem like the kind of salad you'd only order if you were out at a restaurant, but you won't believe how easy it is to make for yourself at home. You'll never need a premade salad mix again!

INGREDIENTS

Dressing and Marinade

⅓ cup honey

2 tablespoons whole-grain mustard

2 tablespoons Dijon mustard

1 small garlic clove, chopped

¼ teaspoon kosher salt

2 tablespoons olive oil

Chicken and Salad

1 pound boneless, skinless chicken breasts

4 cups chopped romaine lettuce, plus a few leaves for garnish

1 cup sliced cucumber

½ cup red and yellow cherry tomatoes, halved

½ cup chopped red onion

4 bacon slices, cooked until crisp, chopped

1 avocado, pitted, peeled, and cut into ½-inch dice

DIRECTIONS

1. *For the dressing and marinade:* Make the dressing/marinade by placing the honey, whole-grain mustard, Dijon mustard, garlic, and salt into a small food processor or blender. Blend and with the machine running, add the olive oil. Set aside.

2. *For the chicken and salad:* Cut the chicken breasts in half horizontally to a ½-inch thickness. Place half of the dressing/marinade in a large zip-top bag and add the chicken. Close the top and use your hands to thoroughly coat the chicken with the marinade. Let it stand at room temperature for 30 minutes or chill until ready to cook.

3. Prepare an outdoor grill or heat a stovetop grill pan over medium-high heat. Lay the chicken on the grill and cook for about 4 minutes per side, until chicken is cooked through.

4. In a large serving bowl, place the lettuce, cucumber, tomatoes, and onion. Toss with the other half of the dressing, reserving 2 tablespoons. Cut the chicken into thin slices and add to the bowl, then top with bacon and avocado. Drizzle with the remaining dressing, if desired. Serve.

Chicken Lettuce Wraps

Yield: Serves 4 | Prep Time: 10 minutes | Cook Time: 30 minutes

Not sure what to make for your gluten-free friend who's coming to visit? These lettuce wraps are a great option! They're just what you need to give yourself a healthy reset after you've indulged in a big meal the night before. Just make sure you get gluten-free hoisin sauce, and then chow down to enjoy!

INGREDIENTS

1 tablespoon vegetable oil

1 pound ground chicken

½ cup shredded carrots

½ cup chopped red and/or green bell pepper

3 garlic cloves, minced

1 (4.9-ounce) can sliced water chestnuts, drained and chopped

¼ cup hoisin sauce

2 tablespoons soy sauce

1 teaspoon sesame oil

1 tablespoon rice vinegar

1 tablespoon grated fresh ginger

2 teaspoons sriracha sauce

4 green onions, thinly sliced

Kosher salt and freshly ground black pepper

1 head butter lettuce (about 6 ounces)

DIRECTIONS

1. In a large skillet, heat the vegetable oil over medium-high heat. Add the ground chicken and cook until browned, for 4–5 minutes. Add the carrots, pepper, and garlic. Cook until the vegetables begin to soften, 5–7 minutes.

2. Add the water chestnuts and stir to combine. Add the hoisin sauce, soy sauce, sesame oil, rice vinegar, ginger, and sriracha sauce. Stir to combine well.

3. Transfer to a serving dish and stir in the green onions, salt, and pepper.

4. To serve, scoop 3–4 tablespoons of the meat mixture into a lettuce leaf. Fold up the leaf and eat.

Barbecue Ranch Grilled Chicken

Yield: Serves 4 | Prep Time: 20 minutes plus 30 minutes marinade time | Cook Time: 8–10 minutes

A little bit hot, a little bit cool, this outdoor chicken is certainly unforgettable! If you prefer something a little spicier, add a bit more barbecue sauce. If you'd like it to be less spicy, add more ranch dressing. Customize it to your taste!

INGREDIENTS

Chicken

4 boneless, skinless chicken breasts

¾ cup ranch salad dressing

¾ cup barbecue sauce

Slaw

4 cups shredded green cabbage

1 cup shredded red cabbage

1 cup very thinly sliced celery

½ cup thinly sliced green bell pepper

½ cup finely diced onion

⅓ cup ranch salad dressing

1 tablespoon red wine vinegar or apple cider vinegar

1 teaspoon celery seed

½ teaspoon kosher salt

DIRECTIONS

1. *For the chicken:* If the chicken breasts are large, cut each in half horizontally to a ½-inch thickness. Place the ranch dressing and barbecue sauce in a large zip-top bag and add the chicken. Close the top and use your hands to thoroughly coat the chicken with the marinade. Let stand at room temperature for 30 minutes or chill until ready to cook.

2. *For the slaw:* While the chicken rests, combine all the slaw ingredients in a large bowl and toss well—using your hands works best—for 1 minute, until every bit is coated with the dressing. Let it stand for 30 minutes to marry the flavors.

3. Prepare an outdoor grill or heat a stovetop grill pan over medium-high heat. Lay the chicken on the grill and cook for 4–5 minutes per side, until chicken is cooked through.

4. Serve the chicken with the slaw on the side.

Chicken Fajita Quesadillas

Yield: Serves 4 | Prep Time: 15 minutes | Cook Time: 45 minutes

Can't decide between fajitas and quesadillas? Now you don't have to! This Mexican mash-up has the best of both worlds—the mix of veggies and spices you crave from fajitas in a convenient, cheesy quesadilla package. What's not to love?

INGREDIENTS

3 tablespoons olive oil

1 teaspoon kosher salt

1 teaspoon freshly ground black pepper

2 tablespoons ground cumin

1 teaspoon chili powder

1 teaspoon garlic powder

1 teaspoon onion powder

1½ pounds boneless, skinless chicken breasts

1 red bell pepper, cut into strips

1 green onion, cut into strips

1 yellow onion, chopped

8 (6-inch) flour tortillas

8 ounces shredded Mexican-blend cheese

1 cup salsa, for serving

DIRECTIONS

1. In a small bowl, combine half of the olive oil with the salt, black pepper, cumin, chili powder, garlic powder, and onion powder. Divide evenly into two bowls. In one bowl, add the chicken and toss with the spices to combine. In the second bowl, add the red pepper, green onion, and yellow onion. Toss with the spices to combine.

2. Heat a large skillet over medium-high heat. Add the remaining olive oil and the chicken to the pan. Cook on each side for 5–7 minutes, until the chicken is cooked through. Remove the chicken to a plate and allow it to rest. Add the vegetables to the pan, cooking until the vegetables begin to soften and start to char slightly, 5–7 minutes. Slice the chicken into 1-inch slices and return to the pan. Stir everything together and remove from the heat.

3. To prepare the quesadillas, heat a medium nonstick skillet over medium heat. Coat lightly with cooking spray. Place one tortilla in the pan, top with one-eighth of the cheese, chicken, and vegetable mixture, another one-eighth of the cheese, and an additional tortilla. Flip the quesadilla when the bottom begins to brown. Cook for an additional 2–3 minutes until the second side is lightly browned. Move to a cutting board and allow it to set for 1 minute. Cut into quarters and repeat with the remaining tortillas. Serve with the salsa.

Chicken, Bacon, and Avocado Panini

Yield: Serves 2 | Prep Time: 10 minutes | Cook Time: 5 minutes

If that panini press (or grill press) from your wedding registry has been gathering dust at the back of the cabinet, it's time to break it out for this classic panini! Paninis don't have to just be for lunch—they're such a quick and easy solution for dinner, too.

INGREDIENTS

4 slices thickly cut sourdough bread

1–2 teaspoons mayonnaise

4 slices Swiss, Monterey Jack, or pepper Jack cheese

1 boneless, skinless chicken breast, cooked and sliced

4 bacon slices, cooked

½ avocado, sliced

Olive oil, for grilling

DIRECTIONS

1. Preheat a panini press or grill pan.

2. Spread one slice of bread with mayonnaise.

3. Layer 1 slice of cheese, half the chicken slices (or as many as you'd like), 2 slices of bacon, half the avocado slices, and top with another slice of cheese before adding the top slice of bread. Repeat for the second sandwich.

4. Drizzle olive oil on both sides of the bread.

5. Place the sandwiches on the panini press or grill pan and press until the bread is golden.

6. If using a grill pan, flip the sandwiches after 2 minutes to grill the other sides. Serve.

NOTES

To cook the chicken, place the breast on a baking sheet and bake at 350°F for 30 minutes.

Soy Sesame Chicken Salad

Yield: Serves 4 | Prep Time: 15 minute plus 1 hour marinade time | Cook Time: 15 minutes

My husband is often skeptical when I tell him that a salad can be a filling meal all on its own. When I made him this chicken salad recipe, he had to relent. With protein and so many different veggies, this is one of those salads that can shine all by itself.

INGREDIENTS

2 boneless, skinless chicken breasts

1 (16-ounce) bottle Asian toasted sesame dressing

1 tablespoon olive oil

1 head romaine lettuce, chopped (about 22 ounces)

1 (10-ounce) can mandarin oranges

2 tomatoes, cut into wedges

4 green onions, sliced on an angle

½ small red onion, halved and thinly sliced

2 celery stalks, chopped

¼ cup shredded carrots

Tuxedo sesame seeds (mixed black and white), for garnish

DIRECTIONS

1. In a large bowl, combine the chicken breasts and ¼ cup of the Asian dressing. Allow them to marinate for up to 1 hour.

2. In a medium skillet, heat the olive oil over medium heat. Add the chicken to the pan. Cook for 5–7 minutes on each side until the chicken is cooked through. Allow the chicken to rest for 5 minutes before slicing into 1-inch strips.

3. To make the salad, toss the romaine lettuce, mandarin oranges, tomatoes, green onions, red onion, celery, and shredded carrots in a large salad bowl. Divide among four plates and top each serving with half a chicken breast on top. Top with additional Asian dressing and sesame seeds.

Weeknight Chicken Tacos

Yield: Serves 6–8 | Prep Time: 15 minutes | Cook Time: 30 minutes

I'll admit it; I used to be a bit intimidated by tacos. You start imagining the grease and chopping all the toppings, and it almost deters you. This twist on the classic taco will make everyone happy and make taco night a welcome addition to the dinnertime rotation.

INGREDIENTS

Chicken

1½ pounds boneless, skinless chicken thighs

½ teaspoon kosher salt

½ teaspoon freshly ground black pepper

2 tablespoons olive oil

2 teaspoons ground cumin

½ teaspoon chili powder

½ teaspoon garlic powder

½ teaspoon onion powder

Pico de Gallo

1 cup cherry tomatoes, quartered

½ red onion, finely diced

¼ cup fresh cilantro, chopped

1 jalapeño, seeded and finely chopped

Juice of 1 lime

Crema

3 tablespoons sour cream

½ cup half-and-half

Zest and juice of ½ lime

⅛ teaspoon kosher salt

8–12 (4-inch) corn tortillas

1 avocado, pitted, peeled, and sliced

4 ounces queso fresco cheese, crumbled

Lime wedges, for garnish

Additional chopped cilantro, for garnish

DIRECTIONS

1. *For the chicken:* Preheat the oven to 350°F. Line a baking sheet with aluminum foil.

2. In a large bowl, combine the chicken, salt, pepper, olive oil, cumin, chili powder, garlic powder, and onion powder. Toss to combine. Spread the chicken in an even layer on the baking sheet and bake for 30 minutes, until the chicken is cooked through.

3. *For the pico de gallo:* Meanwhile, in a medium bowl, combine the cherry tomatoes, red onion, cilantro, jalapeño, and lime juice and place in the refrigerator until serving.

4. *For the crema:* In a small bowl, combine the sour cream, half-and-half, lime zest, lime juice, and salt and whisk to combine. Refrigerate until serving.

5. When the chicken is cooked, remove the baking sheet from the oven and allow the chicken to cool slightly. Shred the meat with two forks or chop into smaller pieces.

6. Warm the corn tortillas by wrapping them in a damp towel and microwaving for 30–40 seconds.

7. To serve, fill a warm tortilla with meat, pico de gallo, and avocado slices. Top the taco with crumbled queso fresco, cilantro, lime juice, and a drizzle of crema.

Grilled Pineapple Teriyaki Chicken

Yield: Serves 4 | Prep Time: 15 minutes | Cook Time: 15 minutes

Bring a little of the tropics into your home! Hawaiian dinner nights are fun to throw during the summer when you're missing the warm, sandy beaches and sea salt in the air. You'll just need to make a fruity drink to serve on the side!

INGREDIENTS

4 boneless, skinless chicken breasts

1 teaspoon chili powder

½ teaspoon kosher salt

¼ teaspoon freshly ground black pepper

1 cup chopped lettuce

¼ red onion, halved and thinly sliced

1 cup pineapple chunks

1 avocado, sliced (optional)

4 (8-inch) flour tortillas

½ cup teriyaki sauce

Sesame seeds, for garnish

DIRECTIONS

1. Preheat a grill pan over medium-high heat.

2. Place the chicken breasts between two sheets of plastic wrap and pound them to a ½-inch thickness. Season the chicken with the chili powder, salt, and pepper.

3. Grill the chicken for 5–8 minutes on each side until fully cooked.

4. Assemble the wraps by placing chicken, lettuce, onion, pineapple, and avocado slices (if using) on each tortilla.

5. Sprinkle with teriyaki sauce and sesame seeds.

Four-Ingredient Chicken

Yield: Serves 4 | Prep Time: 5 minutes | Cook Time: 20 minutes

I love to cook, but some nights, I'm just not in the mood for chopping, dicing, measuring, and so on. I need something quick that I can put together without too much attention, and that's when I come back to this recipe. There's something about a lightly seasoned cheesy chicken dish that just hits the spot. It's so easy I have to restrain myself from cooking it multiple nights a week.

INGREDIENTS

4 boneless, skinless chicken breasts

¼ cup olive oil

1 teaspoon oregano

1 cup mozzarella cheese

Kosher salt and freshly ground black pepper

Thyme and parsley, for garnish (optional)

DIRECTIONS

1. Preheat the oven to 400°F. Line a baking sheet with aluminum foil.

2. Place the chicken breasts in a zip-top bag and pour in the olive oil and oregano. Shake to coat.

3. Place the chicken breasts on the baking sheet and bake for 15 minutes.

4. Remove from the oven and sprinkle with mozzarella cheese to cover.

5. Bake for an additional 5 minutes.

6. Sprinkle with salt and pepper. Garnish with thyme and parsley, if desired. Serve.

Greek Chicken Gyros

Yield: Serves 4–6 | Prep Time: 10 minutes, plus marinade time | Cook Time: 15 minutes

There's something about the way the tangy yogurt combines with the warm, salty chicken that makes gyros such a standout.

INGREDIENTS

Marinade

4 garlic cloves, finely minced

1 tablespoon red-wine vinegar

Juice of ½ lemon

2 tablespoons olive oil

3 tablespoons plain Greek yogurt

2 tablespoons dried oregano

1½ teaspoons kosher salt

1½ teaspoons freshly ground black pepper

2 pounds boneless, skinless chicken thighs, cut into pieces

Tzatziki Sauce

1 English (hothouse) cucumber, grated

1½ cups plain Greek yogurt

2 tablespoons red wine vinegar

2 tablespoons fresh lemon juice

2 tablespoons olive oil

2 garlic cloves, finely minced

1 teaspoon kosher salt

1 teaspoon freshly ground black pepper

Salad

½ red onion, thinly sliced and placed in a bowl of cold water to soak

2 tomatoes, coarsely chopped

1 English (hothouse) cucumber, diced

¼ cup fresh flat-leaf parsley, chopped

4–6 pita or flat breads

DIRECTIONS

1. *For the marinade:* In a large zip-top bag, combine the garlic, red-wine vinegar, lemon juice, olive oil, Greek yogurt, oregano, salt, and pepper. Massage to mix well.

2. Add the chicken, seal the bag, and massage to coat with the marinade. Marinate in the refrigerator for at least 2 hours or up to 12 hours.

3. *For the tzatziki sauce:* Wrap the grated cucumber in a clean kitchen towel. Squeeze well to remove the excess water. Place in a bowl and add the Greek yogurt, red-wine vinegar, lemon juice, olive oil, garlic, salt, and pepper. Mix well. Cover with plastic and refrigerate.

4. *For the salad:* Drain the red onion well and put it in a large bowl. Add the tomatoes, cucumber, and parsley. Mix well.

5. Preheat the broiler to high with an oven rack in the top position. Cover a baking sheet with foil and place a wire rack on top. Spray the wire rack with cooking spray. Remove the chicken from the marinade and place on the rack. Broil for 5–7 minutes, until just beginning to brown. Flip the chicken and cook for 5–7 minutes more. Allow to cool slightly.

6. Place one piece of chicken on each pita. Top with salad and tzatziki sauce. Serve.

Chicken Caesar Salad

Yield: Serves 4 | Prep Time: 5 minutes | Cook Time: 30 minutes

Everyone needs a classic, go-to salad recipe they can rely on for a first course. This one is mine. The cheese and bell pepper add just enough color to keep the dish visually interesting, and its simplicity ensures that even the picky eaters at the table will want a bite.

INGREDIENTS

2 boneless, skinless chicken breasts

Kosher salt and freshly ground black pepper

2 heads romaine lettuce (about 22 ounces)

1 red bell pepper, thinly sliced

½ cup grated Parmesan cheese

2 cups Caesar dressing

Parsley, for garnish

DIRECTIONS

1. Preheat the oven to 350°F. Line a baking sheet with aluminum foil.

2. Place the chicken breasts on the baking sheet and season with salt and pepper. Bake for 30 minutes or until done.

3. Meanwhile, finely chop the romaine lettuce and toss with the bell pepper. Add the Parmesan cheese.

4. Remove the chicken from the oven and allow it to cool for a few minutes. Using a fork and knife, shred the chicken and place in a medium bowl. Cover with the Caesar dressing to coat.

5. Place the chicken on top of the lettuce, garnish with parsley, and serve.

Barbecue Chicken, Bacon, and Pineapple Kabobs

Yield: 6–8 skewers | Prep Time: 20 minutes plus 2–3 hours marinade time | Cook Time: 20 minutes

Kabobs were designed to be the ideal mingling dinner. You just grab a skewer as you wander around catching up with friends, munching as you go, savoring the combination of sweet, tart pineapple against the salty, smoky bacon. It's a must-have at your next block party.

INGREDIENTS

2 large boneless, skinless chicken breasts, cut into 1½–2-inch chunks

1 cup barbecue sauce

1 pound bacon, cut into 1½-inch pieces

1 fresh pineapple, cut into 2-inch chunks

1 red bell pepper, cut into 2-inch chunks

1 green bell pepper, cut into 2-inch chunks

1 red onion, cut into 2-inch chunks

DIRECTIONS

1. Combine the chicken and barbecue sauce in a large zip-top bag and marinate in the refrigerator for 2–3 hours.

2. Soak 6–8 (12-inch) wooden skewers in water for 1 hour.

3. Microwave the bacon for 1–2 minutes or cook on the stovetop until crispy.

4. Thread the chicken, bacon, pineapple, red bell pepper, green bell pepper, and onions onto the skewers in an alternating pattern. It may be necessary to fold the bacon in half to fit it on the skewers.

5. Prepare an outdoor grill. Grill the kabobs over high heat until the chicken and bacon are fully cooked to 160–165°F, about 20 minutes, turning halfway through cooking.

6. Serve hot.

Chicken Macaroni Salad

Yield: Serves 12 | Prep Time: 20 minutes plus 1 hour chilling | Cook Time: 10 minutes

You should never have to decide between bringing pasta salad or chicken salad. You might as well kill two birds (or chickens!) with one stone and just bring both!

INGREDIENTS

1 pound elbow macaroni

Kosher salt

4–6 hard-boiled eggs, chopped

1 cup chopped celery

¼ cup diced red bell pepper

¼ cup thinly sliced green onions

1½ cups mayonnaise

½ cup sour cream

4 boneless, skinless chicken breasts, cooked and cut into chunks (about 4 cups)

1 teaspoon freshly ground black pepper

½ teaspoon dry mustard

DIRECTIONS

1. Bring a large pot of water to a boil. Add the macaroni and salt to taste and cook until al dente. Drain and set aside.

2. In a large bowl, mix the macaroni, eggs, celery, red bell pepper, green onions, mayonnaise, sour cream, chicken, dry mustard, 1 teaspoon salt, and black pepper.

3. Chill for at least 1 hour. Serve.

NOTES

To cook the chicken, place the breasts on a baking sheet and bake at 350°F for 30 minutes.

Taco Lime Grilled Chicken Salad

Yield: Serves 4 | Prep Time: 15 minutes plus 30 minutes marinade time | Cook Time: 8–10 minutes

I love serving this out on the back porch for a relaxing Sunday dinner when the sun stays out until eight o'clock and there's a soft breeze in the air. I put out pitchers of margaritas for the adults and lemonade for the kids and sit back to enjoy the flavorful summer veggie combination of corn and tomatoes, topped with a burst of lime.

INGREDIENTS

Marinade and Chicken

1 tablespoon vegetable oil

2 tablespoons taco seasoning

2 tablespoons tequila

¼ cup fresh lime juice

1 pound boneless, skinless chicken breasts

Salad

2 cups shredded iceberg lettuce

1 cup diced tomato

1 (11-ounce) can Southwestern-style corn with peppers and black beans, drained

½ cup diced red onion

2 tablespoons vegetable oil

2 tablespoons fresh lime juice

2 tablespoons chopped fresh cilantro

1 tablespoon very finely chopped jalapeño (optional)

Kosher salt and freshly ground black pepper

DIRECTIONS

1. *For the marinade and chicken:* Combine the vegetable oil, taco seasoning, tequila, and lime juice in a zip-top bag. Cut the chicken breasts in half horizontally and open like a book at a ½-inch thickness. Add the chicken to the zip-top bag. Close the top and use your hands to thoroughly coat the chicken with the marinade. Let it stand at room temperature for 30 minutes or chill until ready to cook.

2. Prepare an outdoor grill or heat a stovetop grill pan over medium-high heat. Lay the chicken on the grill and cook for about 4 minutes per side, until chicken is cooked through. Thinly slice the chicken.

3. *For the salad:* Combine all the salad ingredients in a large bowl with the chicken and stir to combine.

4. Dish into bowls and serve.

4

Slow Cooker

Slow cooker recipes are perfect for when you know you're
going to be out all day and too tired to cook when you get
home. Plus, they free up oven space, so you can bake a tasty
dessert to accompany dinner at the same time!

Dump 'n' Go Hawaiian Chicken

Yield: Serves 6–8 | Prep Time: 15 minutes | Cook Time: 2–2½ hours on High or 4–5 hours on Low

Put the knives and cutting boards away. This is one of those chicken dishes that couldn't be any simpler. Just throw everything into the slow cooker, and leave it to work its magic. Enjoy that tropical pineapple flavor!

INGREDIENTS

4–5 boneless, skinless chicken breasts (about 2 pounds)

¼ cup cornstarch

½ cup packed light brown sugar

½ cup soy sauce

¼ cup orange marmalade

¼ cup fresh lime juice

2 teaspoons minced or grated fresh ginger

1 teaspoon kosher salt

½ teaspoon freshly ground black pepper

1 (20-ounce) can pineapple chunks, drained

1 (15-ounce) can mandarin oranges, drained

Sprigs of fresh thyme, for garnish

Cooked white rice, for serving

DIRECTIONS

1. Coat a 6-quart slow cooker insert with cooking spray.

2. Place the chicken breasts into the slow cooker.

3. In a medium bowl, whisk together the cornstarch, brown sugar, soy sauce, orange marmalade, lime juice, ginger, salt, and pepper. Pour over the chicken.

4. Add the pineapple and mandarin oranges.

5. Cover and cook for 4–5 hours on Low or for 2–2½ hours on High.

6. Serve over rice. Garnish with thyme.

Russian Chicken

Yield: Serves 4 | Prep Time: 10 minutes | Cook Time: 4 hours

Typically, when you see fruit mixed with chicken, it tends to be something citrusy, like lemons or limes. This recipe is a bit unique in that it uses peaches instead. While this might not be the type of chicken recipe you'd usually try, it'll certainly be one you keep coming back to because the light, sweet fruit mixed with the thick, smooth Russian dressing makes this one a keeper.

INGREDIENTS

2 pounds boneless, skinless chicken breasts or thighs, or a combination

1 cup Russian dressing

1½ cups sliced peeled peaches, fresh or frozen (about 6 ounces)

½ cup peach jam

Cooked white or brown rice, for serving

Parsley, for garnish

DIRECTIONS

1. Coat a 6-quart slow cooker insert with cooking spray.

2. Cut the chicken into 1½-inch-wide strips and place them in the slow cooker in a single layer.

3. In a medium bowl, combine the Russian dressing, peaches, and peach jam, and toss to mix; pour over the chicken in the slow cooker. Cover and cook for 4 hours on Low.

4. Serve over the rice. Garnish with parsley.

Lazy Chicken and Potatoes

Yield: Serves 4 | Prep Time: 10 minutes | Cook Time: 4–6 hours

The foundation to any feel-good dinner recipe has to be some sort of meat-and-potato combination. I generally have to leave the house to run errands when I make this because the combination of potatoes, onions, peppers, and garlic, simmering in the slow cooker all day, smells too incredible to resist.

INGREDIENTS

1½ pounds baby red potatoes, halved

1 yellow onion, cut into chunks (about 1 cup)

1 green bell pepper, cut into strips (about 1 cup)

1 poblano pepper, cut into thin strips

2 tablespoons slivered garlic cloves

1½ pounds boneless, skinless chicken breasts or thighs, or a combination

1 teaspoon ground cumin

½ teaspoon kosher salt

½ cup of barbecue sauce

½ cup tomato or V8 juice, or chicken broth

Parsley, for garnish

DIRECTIONS

1. Coat a 6-quart slow cooker insert with cooking spray.

2. In a large bowl, combine the potatoes, onion, green bell pepper, poblano pepper, and garlic and toss to mix. Pour into the slow cooker. Top with the chicken and sprinkle with the cumin and salt.

3. In a small bowl, combine the barbecue sauce and tomato juice and pour over the slow cooker contents. Cover and cook for 4–6 hours on Low, until the chicken is cooked through. Garnish with parsley and serve.

Slow Cooker Chicken Piccata

Yield: Serves 4 | Prep Time: 15 minutes | Cook Time: 4 hours

This traditional dish is usually made with veal in Italy, but the chicken version has been embraced here in the United States, and I've adapted it for an easy slow cooker version. Serve alongside your favorite sautéed or steamed green vegetable and a glass of wine for a romantic night in.

INGREDIENTS

2 large boneless, skinless chicken breasts (about 1½ pounds)

1 large egg

½ cup dry Italian-flavored bread crumbs

½ teaspoon dried oregano

½ teaspoon kosher salt

¼ teaspoon freshly ground black pepper

1 tablespoon olive oil

1 cup chicken broth

1 cup white wine

⅓ cup fresh lemon juice

1 (6-ounce) jar marinated artichokes, drained

2 tablespoons capers, drained

Cooked linguine, lemon wedges and chopped fresh parsley, for serving

DIRECTIONS

1. Cut the chicken breasts in half horizontally, then slice crosswise in half again, leaving you with four pieces per breast.

2. Beat the egg with 1 tablespoon of water and pour into a pie plate or shallow bowl. Combine the bread crumbs, oregano, salt, and pepper in another pie plate or shallow bowl. Dredge the chicken pieces first in the egg and then in the crumb mixture, patting to coat each piece completely.

3. In a wide, heavy-bottom skillet, heat the olive oil over medium-high heat. Add the chicken and cook until lightly golden brown, about 3 minutes on each side. The chicken may not be completely cooked through—it will continue to cook in the slow cooker.

4. Coat a 6-quart slow cooker insert with cooking spray. Place the chicken in a single layer in the bottom of the slow cooker insert.

5. In the same pan used for the chicken, combine the chicken broth, white wine, and lemon juice and bring to a boil over medium heat, stirring to scrape up any browned bits from the bottom of the pan. Scatter the artichokes and capers over the chicken and pour the broth mixture over the top. Cover and cook for 4 hours on Low.

6. Serve over linguine, garnished with lemon wedges and parsley.

Easy as 1-2-3 Pineapple Chicken

Yield: Serves 4–6 | Prep Time: 15 minutes | Cook Time: 4 hours

Pineapple and brown sugar add a sweet twist to your typical chicken recipe. Along with an umami kick from soy sauce and the subtle acid of rice vinegar, these ingredients make it so easy to add a lot of flavor without all the fuss.

INGREDIENTS

Chicken

1½ pounds boneless, skinless chicken thighs or breasts, cut into 1½-inch cubes

2 tablespoons cornstarch

½ cup diced red bell pepper

½ cup diced red onion

½ cup crushed pineapple packed in pineapple juice, juice reserved

3 tablespoons packed light brown sugar

3 tablespoons soy sauce

1 tablespoon rice vinegar

Rice

1 tablespoon finely diced red bell pepper

1 tablespoon finely diced green bell pepper

1 tablespoon finely diced red onion

1 tablespoon finely diced green onion, including some of the green tops

1 teaspoon sesame oil

1½ cups jasmine or basmati rice

3 cups chicken broth, low-sodium preferred

DIRECTIONS

1. Coat a 6-quart slow cooker insert with cooking spray.

2. *For the chicken:* In a large bowl, combine the chicken and 1 tablespoon cornstarch and stir well until the chicken is coated with the cornstarch. Add the red bell pepper, red onion, pineapple, brown sugar, soy sauce, and rice vinegar and stir. Place the mixture into the slow cooker, cover, and cook for 3¾ hours on Low.

3. In a small bowl, combine the remaining 1 tablespoon cornstarch with ¼ cup of the reserved pineapple juice and stir until smooth. Pour into the slow cooker, stirring well. Cover and cook for an additional 15 minutes on Low.

4. *For the rice:* In a small bowl, combine the red and green bell pepper, red and green onion, and sesame oil and set aside.

5. Cook the rice with the broth according to the package directions. Remove the lid and stir in the diced vegetable mixture, cover, and allow to stand for 5 minutes before serving with the chicken mixture.

Secret Ingredient Chicken and Rice

Yield: Serves 4–6 | Prep Time: 10 minutes | Cook Time: 2–3 hours

If you want to get your kids to actually finish everything on their plate, just tell them that their dinner has soda in it! The lemon-lime soda adds flavor and moisture. Plus, it's a fun way to mix things up while working with your favorite staple dinner ingredients.

INGREDIENTS

3 pounds boneless, skinless chicken breasts

½ teaspoon dried rosemary

½ teaspoon dried thyme

½ teaspoon freshly ground black pepper

1 (10.5-ounce) can cream of mushroom soup

1 (12-ounce) can lemon-lime soda

1 cup white rice

¼ cup chicken broth, low-sodium preferred

1 cup shredded white cheddar cheese

Sprigs of fresh rosemary, for garnish

DIRECTIONS

1. Coat a 6-quart slow cooker insert with cooking spray.

2. Place the chicken in the bottom of the slow cooker.

3. Sprinkle the rosemary, thyme, and pepper over the chicken.

4. Pour the cream of mushroom soup and lemon-lime soda over the top.

5. Cover and cook for 1–1½ hours on High.

6. Add the rice and broth and cook for another 1–1½ hours on High, until the chicken is cooked.

7. In the last 30 minutes of cooking, add the white cheddar cheese and mix.

8. Garnish with rosemary and serve.

Down South Slow Cooker Chicken and Stuffing

Yield: Serves 6 | Prep Time: 15 minutes | Cook Time: 3–4 hours

Yes, you can absolutely have stuffing for dinner when it's not Thanksgiving or Christmas! There's no reason why you should deprive yourself for ten months out of the year when slow cooker recipes like this one are fabulous all year long. The sweet and nutty Jarlsberg cheese adds a unique and festive touch.

INGREDIENTS

4 boneless, skinless chicken breasts, cut into chunks

½ teaspoon kosher salt

½ teaspoon freshly ground black pepper

½ teaspoon poultry seasoning

6 slices Jarlsberg cheese

1 (10.5-ounce) can cream of chicken soup

1 (10.5-ounce) can cream of celery soup

½ cup half-and-half

½ cup sour cream

1 (6-ounce) box chicken or herb stuffing mix

½ cup (1 stick) unsalted butter, melted

Parsley, for garnish

DIRECTIONS

1. Coat a 6-quart slow cooker insert with cooking spray.

2. Season the chicken with the salt, pepper, and poultry seasoning.

3. Place the chicken in the bottom of the slow cooker.

4. Cover the chicken with the Jarlsberg cheese slices.

5. In a medium bowl, combine the cream of chicken soup, cream of celery soup, half-and-half, and sour cream.

6. Pour the soup mixture over the cheese slices.

7. Sprinkle the dry stuffing mix on top of the soup mixture and then drizzle the melted butter on top.

8. Cover and cook for 3–4 hours on High. Garnish with parsley and serve.

Outrageous Cashew Chicken

Yield: Serves 6–8 | Prep Time: 10 minutes | Cook Time: 3 hours

Add a little crunch to your dinner with a nutty chicken recipe. This takeout specialty blends together all your favorite flavors like soy sauce, sweet chili sauce, and ginger.

INGREDIENTS

½ cup soy sauce

2 tablespoons rice vinegar

3 tablespoons sweet chili sauce

1 teaspoon sesame oil

¼ teaspoon red pepper flakes

1½ pounds boneless, skinless chicken thighs, cut into 1½-inch cubes

2 tablespoons cornstarch

½ teaspoon freshly ground white pepper

1 tablespoon peanut oil

1½ teaspoons finely minced garlic

1½ teaspoons finely minced ginger

3–4 green onions, sliced into 1-inch pieces, plus 2 tablespoons thinly sliced green onion tops, for garnish

1 cup roasted cashews

DIRECTIONS

1. Coat a 6-quart slow cooker insert with cooking spray and set aside.

2. *For the sauce:* In a small bowl, combine the soy sauce, rice vinegar, sweet chili sauce, sesame oil, and red pepper flakes and set near the stove.

3. *For the chicken:* In a large bowl, combine the chicken cubes, cornstarch, and white pepper, tossing with a fork or your hands to be sure the chicken is well coated.

4. In a wok or large skillet, heat the peanut oil over high heat until the oil shimmers. Add the garlic, ginger, and green onions and constantly toss and stir until fragrant, about 30 seconds. Add the chicken and continue to toss and stir until the chicken is lightly browned, about 1 minute. The chicken does not have to be completely cooked at this point.

5. Add the prepared sauce to the pan and stir until it bubbles. Pour the chicken and sauce into the prepared slow cooker, cover, and cook for 3 hours on Low.

6. Just before serving, add the roasted cashews and stir. Garnish with green onions and serve.

Mango Salsa Slow Cooker Chicken

Yield: Serves 4 | Prep Time: 10 minutes | Cook Time: 4 hours

This six-ingredient dinner recipe is so simple to throw together that it may become a weekly regular. Mangoes have two peak seasons, making them available all year long, so you'll never have to worry about your grocery store being out of stock.

INGREDIENTS

½ cup sliced red onion

1 (16-ounce) jar thick chunky salsa

1 pound boneless, skinless chicken breasts or thighs

1 large mango, seeded, peeled, and sliced

2 tablespoons honey

Cooked rice, for serving

Grape tomatoes, for garnish

Parsley, for garnish

DIRECTIONS

1. Coat a 6-quart slow cooker insert with cooking spray. Place the onion on the bottom of the slow cooker and spoon on half the salsa. Arrange the chicken in a single layer on top and spoon the remaining salsa over, covering the chicken. Lay the mango slices over the top, cover, and cook for 4 hours on High.

2. Remove the chicken, leaving the mango in the slow cooker, and place on a serving platter. Add the honey to the slow cooker and use a fork to mix and partially mash the mango into the sauce. Spoon the sauce over the chicken, garnish with grape tomatoes and parsley, and serve with the rice.

Lemon Pepper Chicken Breasts

Yield: Serves 2–4 | Prep Time: 10 minutes | Cook Time: 3–4 hours

The slightly smoky, slightly tart flavor of this lemon pepper dish makes for a lighter dinner recipe that you could enjoy any night of the week. I like serving it alongside freshly steamed broccoli for a healthy weeknight meal.

INGREDIENTS

½ cup all-purpose flour

2 teaspoons freshly ground black pepper, plus more as needed

4 boneless, skinless chicken breasts

4 tablespoons (½ stick) unsalted butter

2 tablespoons olive oil

½ cup white wine

½ cup chicken broth, low-sodium preferred

½ cup fresh lemon juice

1 (1.5-ounce) package dry Italian dressing mix

Lemon rounds, for garnish

Broccoli, for serrving

DIRECTIONS

1. Coat a 6-quart slow cooker insert with cooking spray. In a shallow dish, combine the flour and pepper. Dredge each chicken breast in the flour mixture and set aside.

2. In a large skillet, melt the butter with the olive oil over medium heat. Add the chicken and cook each side for about 4 minutes. You are not cooking the meat through, just lightly browning each side.

3. Transfer the chicken to the slow cooker. In the same skillet, still over medium heat, add the wine and scrape up any browned bits from the bottom of the pan. Bring to a simmer and reduce the liquid, about 5 minutes. Add the chicken broth, and lemon juice. Return to a simmer and cook about 5 minutes.

4. Sprinkle the Italian dressing mix over the chicken. Pour the broth mixture over the top.

5. Cover and cook for 3–4 hours on Low.

6. Serve one or two breasts per person, drizzle with sauce from the slow cooker. Garnish with lemon rounds and serve with broccoli.

5

Skillet

Who knew you could use just one skillet to make such
a bounty of chicken dishes? Skillets and chicken go hand in
hand to create some of the tastiest dishes ever. From five-star
restaurant-style favorites to recipes that have been around for
generations, there's almost nothing you can't make in a skillet.

Cheesy Chicken and Rice

Yield: Serves 4 | Prep Time: 5 minutes | Cook Time: 35 minutes

I love finding innovative ways to use canned soups in dinner recipes. They're so inexpensive at the grocery store that I make a habit of stocking up on a whole bunch to keep in my pantry for a rainy day.

INGREDIENTS

1 tablespoon vegetable oil

4 boneless, skinless chicken breasts

1 (10.5-ounce) can cream of chicken soup

½ teaspoon onion powder

¼ teaspoon freshly ground black pepper

1 cup long-grain white rice

2 cups frozen mixed vegetables

½ cup shredded cheddar cheese

Fresh parsley, for garnish

DIRECTIONS

1. In a medium skillet, heat the vegetable oil over medium-high heat. Add the chicken and cook for 10 minutes, flipping the chicken halfway through, or until well browned on both sides. Remove the chicken from the skillet.

2. In the same skillet, stir together the cream of chicken soup, 1½ cups of water, onion powder, pepper, and white rice and bring to a boil. Reduce the heat to low. Cover and cook for 15 minutes, stirring once halfway through the cooking time.

3. Stir in the frozen mixed vegetables. Return the chicken to the skillet and sprinkle with the cheese. Cover and cook for 5 minutes, or until the chicken is cooked through and the rice is tender. Garnish with parsley and serve.

Chicken Fried Rice

Yield: Serves 6–8 | Prep Time: 15 minutes | Cook Time: 10 minutes

Chicken fried rice is such an adaptable recipe. If you have certain veggies that you love, throw them in! Never really cared for broccoli? Skip it! It's all up to you to make this dish perfectly suited to your taste.

INGREDIENTS

1 teaspoon olive oil

1 pound boneless, skinless chicken breasts, cooked and shredded

3 cups cooked long-grain brown rice

1 (16-ounce) bag frozen mixed vegetables

¼ cup low-sodium soy sauce

3 tablespoons rice vinegar

2 large eggs

2 cups cooked broccoli florets

2 green onions, thinly sliced

Kosher salt and freshly ground black pepper

DIRECTIONS

1. In a wok or large skillet, heat the olive oil over high heat. Add the cooked chicken, brown rice, and frozen vegetables. Stir constantly until warmed through, about 5 minutes.

2. Add the soy sauce and vinegar, stirring to combine well. Once well combined, push all of the mixture to the sides, leaving a clear space in the middle of the pan. Crack the eggs into the space and immediately stir them separately in the middle of the pan. Once the eggs are cooked, add the cooked broccoli and green onions.

3. Stir everything together, season with salt and pepper, and serve.

NOTES

To cook the chicken, place the breasts on a baking sheet and bake at 350°F for 30 minutes.

General Tso's Chicken

Yield: Serves 4 | Prep Time: 15 minutes | Cook Time: 15 minutes

This takeout dish is always in high demand in the United States. People just can't get enough of it! Funny thing is, the Chinese general it's named after had nothing to do with its creation. I don't know who to thank for creating this chicken—all I know is that it's incredible.

INGREDIENTS

5 tablespoons cornstarch

2 tablespoons reduced-sodium soy sauce

2 tablespoons Chinese rice wine

1 egg white

1 pound boneless, skinless chicken breasts, cut into 1-inch pieces

2 tablespoons hoisin sauce

1 tablespoon rice vinegar

1 tablespoon honey

1 teaspoon minced or grated fresh ginger

3 tablespoons canola oil

2 garlic cloves, minced

1 pound green beans, trimmed

1 teaspoon sesame seeds

Cooked white or brown rice, for serving

DIRECTIONS

1. In a medium bowl, mix 4 tablespoons of the cornstarch, 1 tablespoon of the soy sauce, 1 tablespoon of the rice wine, and the egg white.

2. Add the chicken and stir to coat.

3. In a separate small bowl, combine the remaining 1 tablespoon each of the cornstarch, soy sauce, and rice wine with ¾ cup of water, the hoisin sauce, rice vinegar, honey, and ginger.

4. In a wok or large skillet, heat 2 tablespoons of the canola oil over high heat. Add the chicken and cook on one side until golden, about 2 minutes. Turn the chicken over and cook the other side for about 2 minutes, until golden. Transfer the chicken to a plate.

5. To the same pan, add the remaining oil along with the garlic. Cook for 15–20 seconds, until garlic is lightly browned.

6. Add the green beans and cook for 3–4 minutes until bright green.

7. Add the reserved sauce mixture, stir, and cook until the sauce has thickened, about 1 minute.

8. Return the chicken to the pan, stir, and cook for an additional 1–2 minutes, until coated.

9. Sprinkle the sesame seeds on top, transfer to a serving dish, and serve with rice.

Extra-Crispy Fried Chicken

Yield: Serves 3 | Prep Time: 15 minutes | Cook Time: 20–25 minutes

If you're looking to emulate prized Southern cooking, this is the dish to start with. Pair this with buttermilk biscuits, mashed potatoes, and corn on the cob, and you've got yourself a truly heavenly meal.

INGREDIENTS

½ cup buttermilk

1 large egg

1 (3–3½-pound) chicken, cut into 8–10 pieces

1 cup all-purpose flour

1 tablespoon kosher salt

1 teaspoon freshly ground black pepper

1 teaspoon paprika

1 teaspoon garlic powder

⅛ teaspoon cayenne pepper

3 cups vegetable oil

DIRECTIONS

1. In a large bowl, combine the buttermilk and egg.

2. Add the chicken pieces and coat well.

3. In another large bowl, combine the flour, salt, black pepper, paprika, garlic powder, and cayenne pepper.

4. Take the chicken from the buttermilk mixture and place in the flour mixture, coating each piece of chicken completely.

5. In a large Dutch oven or deep skillet, heat the vegetable oil until the temperature reaches 350°F.

6. Carefully add the chicken pieces to the oil and fry for 20–25 minutes, until the chicken is browned and fully cooked.

7. Place the cooked chicken on a wire rack set over a baking sheet to cool. Serve.

Old-Fashioned Chicken

Yield: Serves 4 | Prep Time: 20 minutes | Cook Time: 60–70 minutes

When you're tired of trying to make the newest, trendiest dish you see on the Internet, you can always rely on classics like this Old-Fashioned Chicken. With a diverse mix of vegetables combined with juicy chicken thighs, you can't go wrong with my grandma's preferred way to serve chicken.

INGREDIENTS

2 tablespoons olive oil

2½ pounds boneless, skinless chicken thighs

½ teaspoon kosher salt

1 yellow onion, chopped

2 garlic cloves, minced

1 (14-ounce) can cannellini beans, drained

1 pound Yukon Gold potatoes, peeled and cut into bite-size cubes

1 (28-ounce) can fire-roasted tomatoes, undrained

2 tablespoons tomato paste

1 tablespoon fresh thyme, minced, plus extra for garnish

¼ teaspoon red pepper flakes

DIRECTIONS

1. In a large pot or deep skillet, heat the olive oil over medium heat.

2. Sprinkle the chicken with the salt and place in the pot.

3. Sear the chicken and cook for about 10 minutes, browning on both sides.

4. Add the onion and garlic and cook for 2–3 minutes, until softened.

5. Add in the cannellini beans, Yukon Gold potatoes, fire-roasted tomatoes and their juice, tomato paste, thyme, and red pepper flakes.

6. Bring to a boil, then reduce to a simmer. Cook for 45–55 minutes, until the chicken and potatoes are tender and fully cooked. Garnish with thyme and serve.

Chicken à la King in a Hurry

Yield: Serves 4 | Prep Time: 5 minutes | Cook Time: 7 minutes

This may be a "vintage" recipe, famous in tearooms around the country since the 1940s, but we guarantee you and your guests will love it and be glad you've brought it back to the present.

INGREDIENTS

2 tablespoons unsalted butter or olive oil

2 tablespoons finely diced red bell pepper

2 tablespoons finely diced celery

4 ounces white button mushrooms, chopped

½ teaspoon dried thyme

½ teaspoon kosher salt

¼ teaspoon freshly ground black pepper

1 (10.5-ounce) can cream of mushroom soup

½ cup heavy cream, half-and-half, or whole milk

2 boneless, skinless chicken breasts, cooked and cut into ½-inch cubes

1 cup frozen peas, thawed

4 biscuits from a can of refrigerated jumbo biscuits, baked

DIRECTIONS

1. In a large nonstick skillet, melt the butter over medium-high heat. Add the bell pepper and celery and sauté for 1 minute, then add the mushrooms, thyme, salt, and pepper. Cook, stirring frequently, until the mushrooms release their juices and begin to brown lightly, about 4 minutes.

2. Add the cream of mushroom soup, cream, chicken, and peas and stir over medium heat until warmed through, about 2 minutes.

3. Serve immediately with biscuits.

NOTES

To cook the chicken, place the breasts on a baking sheet and bake at 350°F for 30 minutes.

Chicken Francese

Yield: Serves 4 | Prep Time: 15 minutes | Cook Time: 12–14 minutes

I have a cousin who's a really picky eater. When we're at a restaurant, she'll always search for the spaghetti and meatballs or the chicken tenders, just to play it safe. Whenever she comes over to visit, I try to expand her taste buds a bit with something more sophisticated, like this Chicken Francese. It has just enough flavor to satisfy everyone else, but it's not so adventurous as to scare her away.

INGREDIENTS

½ cup all-purpose flour

½ teaspoon kosher salt

¼ teaspoon freshly ground black pepper

2 large eggs

½ cup panko bread crumbs

¼ cup chopped fresh parsley

¼ teaspoon paprika

4 boneless, skinless chicken breasts

3 tablespoons unsalted butter

⅔ cup chicken broth, low-sodium preferred

¼ cup fresh lemon juice

Lemon wheels and fresh parsley, for garnish

DIRECTIONS

1. In a shallow dish or pie plate, combine the flour, salt, and pepper. In another shallow dish or pie plate, beat the eggs and 1 tablespoon of water. In a third shallow dish or pie plate, combine the panko, parsley, and paprika.

2. Place the chicken breasts between two sheets of plastic wrap and pound them to a ⅓-inch thickness. Dip each piece into the flour mixture to cover completely, then into the egg mixture to coat, and finally into the crumb mixture to coat completely. Set aside until the skillet is hot or chill for 30 minutes before proceeding. Reserve the flour mixture.

3. In a wide, shallow skillet, melt 2 tablespoons of the butter over medium-high heat and brown the coated chicken pieces for about 4 minutes per side, until golden brown and nearly cooked through. Transfer to a warm plate.

4. Add the remaining 1 tablespoon butter to the pan and swirl until the butter just begins to turn golden brown. Add 2 tablespoons of the reserved dredging flour and stir with a whisk for 1 minute. Add the broth and lemon juice and stir constantly until reduced to a medium-thick sauce. Taste and adjust the seasoning as needed. Return the chicken to the pan and cook for an additional 2 minutes, or until the chicken is completely cooked.

5. Serve with the sauce poured over the chicken and garnished with lemon wheels and parsley.

Luscious Lemon Chicken

Yield: Serves 4 │ Prep Time: 10 minutes │ Cook Time: 12–15 minutes

I always come back to this recipe around springtime. There's something about adding a hint of lemon that adds a burst of sunshine to my day. Sometimes I'll even make extra to reheat at work for lunch!

INGREDIENTS

2 tablespoons cornstarch

¼ cup fresh lemon juice

Zest of 1 lemon

1½ cups chicken broth, low-sodium preferred

2 teaspoons grated fresh ginger

1 small garlic clove, finely minced

¼ cup packed light brown sugar

2 egg whites

½ cup all-purpose flour

½ cup cornmeal

1 pound boneless, skinless chicken thighs

2 tablespoons olive oil

Cooked white rice, for serving

Chopped green onions, for garnish

Lemon wheels, for garnish

DIRECTIONS

1. In a small bowl, mix the cornstarch with the lemon juice.

2. In a small saucepan, add the lemon zest, chicken broth, ginger, garlic, and brown sugar. Stir in the cornstarch mixture.

3. Bring to a boil and cook for 2–3 minutes, until slightly thickened. Set aside while preparing the chicken. The sauce will thicken as it cools.

4. In another small bowl, whisk together the egg whites and 2 tablespoons of water.

5. In a shallow dish or pie plate, mix together the flour and cornmeal.

6. Dip the chicken in the egg white mixture, and then in the flour mixture to coat evenly.

7. In a large skillet, heat the olive oil over medium-high heat. Fry the chicken pieces until they're golden and the juices run clear, 10–12 minutes.

8. Pour the lemon sauce over the chicken, serve with the white rice, and garnish with chopped green onions and lemon wheels.

One-Pot Cowboy Chicken

Yield: Serves 6 | Prep Time: 20 minutes | Cook Time: 45 minutes

The one thing I don't like about cooking is having to clean up all those dishes after I'm full and ready to take a nap. Sometimes I'll try to clean as I cook, but other times, I'll just stick with a one-pot meal like this to make cleanup a breeze.

INGREDIENTS

2 pounds boneless, skinless chicken breasts

1 tablespoon vegetable oil

½ cup chopped onion

2 tablespoons minced garlic

½ teaspoon kosher salt

1 teaspoon ground cumin

1 tablespoon chopped chipotle chile in adobo sauce

1½ cups white rice

2 (15-ounce) cans chicken broth, low-sodium preferred

2 (11-ounce) cans Southwest Mix vegetables with black beans, corn, and peppers

Sprigs of fresh cilantro, for garnish

DIRECTIONS

1. Pound the chicken breasts until they are ½ inch thick and cut them into thirds crosswise.

2. In a large, deep nonstick skillet, heat the vegetable oil over medium-high heat. Add the chicken and cook for about 3 minutes per side until golden brown. Transfer to a plate and set aside.

3. In the same skillet, cook the onion, stirring often, until it becomes translucent, about 3 minutes. Add the garlic, salt, and cumin and stir for an additional minute. Add the chipotle chile to the sauce and then the rice. Cook, stirring, until the rice begins to turn translucent, about 3 minutes.

4. Return the chicken to the pan, add the broth, and bring to a boil. Lower the heat to medium-low, cover, and cook until the liquid has been absorbed and the rice is nearly cooked, about 20 minutes.

5. Remove the cover, add the Southwest Mix vegetables to the pan, and cook for an additional 10 minutes until heated through.

6. Garnish with cilantro and serve.

Wine-Glazed Chicken

Yield: Serves 4 | Prep Time: 10 minutes | Cook Time: 35 minutes

When cooking with wine, you usually can't go wrong with a crisp white like an unoaked Chardonnay, Pinot Grigio, or Sauvignon Blanc. Plus, as long as you already have the bottle open, you may as well pour yourself a glass, right?

INGREDIENTS

1 teaspoon kosher salt

½ teaspoon freshly ground black pepper

8 bone-in, skin-on chicken thighs

2 tablespoons unsalted butter

2 tablespoons olive oil

1⅓ cups dry white wine

1 cup fresh mushrooms, sliced

1 red bell pepper, thinly sliced

3 green onions, chopped

1 tablespoon fresh rosemary, finely chopped, plus sprigs for garnish

Cooked white or brown rice, for serving

2 tablespoons chicken broth, low-sodium preferred

4 teaspoons cornstarch

DIRECTIONS

1. Season the chicken with salt and pepper.

2. In a large skillet, melt the butter with the olive oil. Add the chicken and cook for 10 minutes until golden on both sides.

3. Stir in the white wine, mushrooms, red bell pepper, green onions, and rosemary. Bring to a boil, then reduce the heat to medium-low. Cover and cook for 20 minutes, or until the chicken is fully cooked.

4. Remove the chicken from the skillet, reserving the drippings, and place the chicken on a plate with warm rice.

5. Whisk together the chicken broth and cornstarch and add it to the drippings in the skillet. Cook until thickened, about 1 minute. Spoon the glaze over the chicken. Garnish with rosemary sprigs and serve.

One-Pot Chicken Cacciatore

Yield: Serves 4 | Prep Time: 15–20 minutes | Cook Time: 40–45 minutes

Chicken cacciatore is often served alongside pasta or with crusty bread, but I love eating it as is since it's already a rather filling meal. This traditional French dinner is easy enough to make during the week but fancy enough to prepare for company.

INGREDIENTS

½ cup all-purpose flour

1 teaspoon kosher salt

¼ teaspoon freshly ground black pepper

2½ pounds boneless, skinless chicken breasts, cut into chunks

4 tablespoons olive oil

1 pound fresh mushrooms, thickly sliced

1 red bell pepper, chopped

1 onion, chopped

2 garlic cloves, minced

1 cup chicken broth, low-sodium preferred

¾ cup dry white wine

1 (28-ounce) jar marinara sauce

1 (28-ounce) can diced tomatoes, undrained

1 teaspoon dried Italian seasoning

Cooked white rice, for serving

Fresh basil, for garnish

DIRECTIONS

1. In a shallow dish or pie plate, combine the flour, ½ teaspoon of the salt, and the black pepper.

2. Add the chicken chunks and coat well.

3. In a large soup pot or deep skillet, heat 3 tablespoons of the olive oil over medium heat until shimmering.

4. Add the chicken and cook until brown on all sides, about 8 minutes. Transfer to a plate.

5. Add the remaining 1 tablespoon olive oil to the pot and add the mushrooms, red bell pepper, onion, and garlic. Cook for 5 minutes, until the onion is translucent.

6. Add the chicken broth, white wine, marinara sauce, diced tomatoes, Italian seasoning, and remaining ½ teaspoon salt.

7. Stir in the chicken and bring to a boil. Reduce the heat to low and simmer for 30–35 minutes, until heated through.

8. Stir and serve over white rice, garnished with basil leaves.

Classic Chicken Schnitzel

Yield: Serves 4 | Prep Time: 20 minutes | Cook Time: 15 minutes

It may look like this recipe has a lot of ingredients, but when you take a closer look, you'll notice that you've got most of these ingredients already lying around in your cupboard at home. This traditional German recipe is simple enough to whip up any time!

INGREDIENTS

Chicken

1 large egg

1 cup fine dry bread crumbs

½ cup grated Parmesan cheese

2 teaspoons finely minced garlic

½ teaspoon kosher salt

¼ teaspoon freshly ground black pepper

4 boneless, skinless chicken breasts

2 tablespoons vegetable oil

Cabbage

1 tablespoon vegetable oil

4 cups finely shredded red cabbage

2 cups finely sliced red onion

½ teaspoon caraway seeds

½ teaspoon sugar

Kosher salt

½ cup chicken broth, low-sodium preferred

1 teaspoon red wine vinegar, plus more as needed

Chopped fresh parsley, for garnish

DIRECTIONS

1. *For the chicken:* Beat the egg with 1 tablespoon of water and pour into a pie plate or shallow bowl. Combine the bread crumbs, Parmesan cheese, garlic, salt, and pepper in another pie plate or shallow bowl.

2. Pound the chicken breasts between sheets of plastic wrap until they're not more than ½ inch thick. Dredge the chicken first in the egg and then in the crumb mixture, patting with your fingers until each piece is evenly and completely coated.

3. In a large, deep skillet, heat the oil over medium-high heat. Add the chicken and cook until golden brown and cooked through, about 4 minutes per side. Remove from the pan and keep warm.

4. *For the cabbage:* In the same skillet, heat the oil over medium heat. Add the cabbage and red onion and cook, tossing for 1 minute. Add the caraway seeds, sugar, and ¼ teaspoon salt and cook, stirring, for about 4 minutes, until onion is softened. Add the chicken broth, partially cover the pan, and cook until the cabbage is tender, about 3 minutes more. Remove the lid and add the red wine vinegar, stirring until the liquids have almost completely evaporated. Taste and add salt or vinegar to balance the flavors. Garnish with parsley and serve.

Chicken, Broccoli, and Mushroom Stir-Fry

Yield: Serves 4–6 | Prep Time: 20 minutes | Cook Time: 8 minutes

This recipe tastes like it came from your favorite takeout spot, but it's even quicker to make than waiting for delivery! Be sure to prepare everything ahead of time, including a pot of rice for serving. All of the ingredients should be arranged near the stove, then quickly stir-fry and enjoy!

INGREDIENTS

2 garlic cloves

1 (1-inch) piece fresh ginger, peeled

1 pound boneless, skinless chicken thighs or breasts, cut into bite-size pieces

1 tablespoon plus 2 teaspoons cornstarch

1 tablespoon soy sauce

2 teaspoons rice vinegar

1 teaspoon sesame oil

8 ounces broccoli, cut into bite-size florets

1 (6-ounce) package snow peas

2 tablespoons vegetable or peanut oil

3 green onions, cut on an angle into ½-inch slices, including some tender green tops, for garnish

4 ounces button mushrooms, stemmed and sliced

1 cup chicken broth, low-sodium preferred

Cooked white rice, for serving

DIRECTIONS

1. Crush and mince the garlic and ginger into a paste. Set 1 tablespoon aside and place the remainder in a medium bowl. Add the chicken, 1 tablespoon of the cornstarch, the soy sauce, vinegar, and sesame oil. Toss well to coat; set aside to marinate for about 10 minutes.

2. Place the broccoli florets and snow peas into a microwaveable container and add 4 tablespoons water. Cover and microwave for 3–5 minutes on high or until crisp, tender, and bright green. Remove the cover and drain.

3. In a small bowl, combine the remaining 2 teaspoons cornstarch and 1 tablespoon of water into a smooth paste. Arrange all the ingredients near the stove. In a wok or large skillet, heat 1 tablespoon of the vegetable oil over medium-high heat. Add the reserved garlic-ginger paste and the green onion, tossing constantly until the oil is fragrant, about 1 minute.

4. Add the chicken and let it cook for 1 minute, then toss and stir for an additional 2 minutes. With a slotted spoon, transfer the chicken to a bowl. Add the remaining vegetable oil to the pan and stir-fry the mushrooms for 1–2 minutes, then add the cooked broccoli and stir-fry for another minute.

5. Return the chicken to the pan, add the chicken broth, and bring to a boil. Stir in the cornstarch mixture and continue to cook and stir until the sauce has thickened, about 2–4 minutes.

6. Serve over white rice, garnished with a few slivers of green onion.

Chicken Lo Mein

Yield: Serves 4 | Prep Time: 15 minutes | Cook Time: 25 minutes

Fresh egg noodles (preferably about ¼-inch thick) are best for making your own lo mein at home. Just keep in mind they need to be softened in boiling water before cooking. Angel-hair pasta makes an excellent substitute.

INGREDIENTS

4 ounces angel-hair pasta

2 teaspoons cornstarch

¼ cup low-sodium soy sauce

2 tablespoons rice vinegar

2 tablespoons hoisin sauce

1 teaspoon sesame oil

1 tablespoon minced fresh gingerroot

1 teaspoon minced garlic

2 tablespoons vegetable or canola oil

1 pound boneless, skinless chicken breasts, cut into strips

1 cup snow peas or snap peas

1 cup julienned carrots

1 red pepper, julienned

¼ cup salted cashews (optional)

DIRECTIONS

1. Bring a large pot of water to a boil. Add the pasta and cook until al dente. Drain and set aside.

2. In a small bowl, whisk together the cornstarch, soy sauce, rice vinegar, hoisin sauce, sesame oil, gingerroot, and garlic.

3. In a large skillet, heat 1 tablespoon of the vegetable oil. Add the chicken and cook for 6–9 minutes until no longer pink. With a slotted spoon, transfer the chicken to a plate.

4. In the same skillet, heat the remaining 1 tablespoon oil. Add the peas, carrots, and red pepper. Cook until crisp-tender, 5–7 minutes.

5. Add the cornstarch mixture to the pan and bring to a boil. Stir for 2–3 minutes until the sauce has thickened.

6. Add the chicken and the pasta and cook until heated through.

7. Sprinkle with the cashews, if using. Serve.

Drunken Chicken with Tomatoes

Yield: Serves 4 | Prep Time: 10 minutes | Cook Time: 25 minutes

This recipe might be the ideal weeknight dish. From start to finish, it'll take you under 45 minutes to make, which leaves you more time to catch up on your favorite TV shows, read a book, or just chill out.

INGREDIENTS

1½ pounds boneless, skinless chicken breasts

⅓ cup all-purpose flour

½ teaspoon poultry seasoning or Italian seasoning

½ teaspoon kosher salt

2 tablespoons olive oil

8 ounces button or cremini mushrooms, sliced

1 tablespoon minced garlic

1 cup Marsala wine

1 teaspoon cornstarch

1 cup whole grape tomatoes

2 tablespoons fresh flat-leaf parsley

DIRECTIONS

1. Cut the chicken breasts in half horizontally and open like a book to make them ½ inch thick. Cut into 8 serving-size pieces. In a large zip-top bag, combine the flour, poultry seasoning, and salt and add the chicken. Close the top and use your hands to thoroughly coat the chicken with the flour mixture.

2. In a large, deep skillet, heat 1 tablespoon of the olive oil over medium-high heat and sauté the chicken until just golden brown, about 3 minutes on each side. Remove the chicken from the pan and side aside on a plate.

3. In the same pan, heat the remaining olive oil. Add the mushrooms and garlic and cook, stirring often, for 6–8 minutes until beginning to brown. Add the Marsala wine and stir until about half of the liquid has evaporated, 4–5 minutes. Mix the cornstarch with 1 tablespoon of water and add to the pan, stirring until well mixed.

4. Chope 1 tablespoon of the parsley.

5. Return the chicken to the pan, top with the tomatoes and the chopped parsley, and simmer for 3–4 minutes, stirring occasionally. Garnish with the remaining parsley and serve.

Chicken Curry

Yield: Serves 4 | Prep Time: 10 minutes | Cook Time: 20 minutes

Dare to try something new! If you've never made Indian food at home before, now's your chance to broaden your horizons and see how easy it is to explore other cuisines.

INGREDIENTS

1 pound boneless, skinless chicken thighs, cut into 1½-inch cubes

1½ teaspoons curry powder (see note)

½ teaspoon kosher salt

¼ teaspoon cayenne pepper, plus more as needed

1 tablespoon vegetable oil

1 cup chopped onion

1 tablespoon finely minced garlic

1 tablespoon finely minced fresh ginger

1 tablespoon cornstarch

2 cups chicken broth, low-sodium preferred

1 teaspoon honey, plus more as needed

1 cup frozen peas, thawed

½ cup plain yogurt

Cooked basmati rice, for serving

Chopped fresh parsley, for garnish

DIRECTIONS

1. Put the chicken in a medium bowl and add the curry powder, salt, and cayenne pepper. Toss until all the spices completely coat the chicken. Let stand while assembling the remaining ingredients.

2. When ready to cook, heat the vegetable oil in a large, deep skillet over medium-high heat. Cook the chicken in the hot oil until partially cooked and nicely browned on all sides, about 8 minutes. Use a slotted spoon to transfer the chicken to a clean bowl. In the same pan, sauté the onion, stirring, until the onion is translucent, about 2 minutes. Add the garlic and ginger and cook, stirring, until very fragrant, 1 minute.

3. In a small bowl, dissolve the cornstarch in 2 tablespoons of the chicken broth, stirring until smooth. Add the remaining chicken broth and the cornstarch mixture to the skillet and stir, scraping up any browned bits from the bottom of the pan with a spoon, and bring to a boil. Reduce the heat to medium, add the honey, and cook, whisking, until the sauce has thickened, 5 minutes. Return the chicken to the pan and add the peas. Cook, stirring frequently, for an additional 2 minutes, or until the chicken is completely cooked. Taste and adjust the flavors as necessary (see notes).

4. Remove the pan from the heat. Using a whisk, stir in the yogurt until smooth. Serve over basmati rice. Garnish with parsley.

NOTES

Commercially available curry powders are premixed blends sold in a wide variety of flavors. If possible, buy from an ethnic grocer or specialty store. Some curry will be sweeter while others will be spicier—just before serving, taste the sauce and adjust the amount of cayenne and honey to achieve a nice balance of flavor.

Kung Pao Chicken

Yield: Serves 5 | Prep Time: 15 minutes | Cook Time: 15 minutes

If you want to go all out, be sure to serve Chicken Egg Rolls (page 9) and even Chicken Fried Rice (page 106) alongside this recipe! And don't be intimidated: unlike some restaurant versions, this has only a hint of spice.

INGREDIENTS

2 tablespoons olive oil

1½ pounds boneless, skinless chicken thighs, trimmed of fat and cut into chunks

1 red bell pepper, diced

1 yellow bell pepper, diced

1 orange bell pepper, diced

2 green onions, thinly sliced

2 garlic cloves, minced

1 tablespoon minced fresh ginger

9 ounces snow peas

1 teaspoon red pepper flakes

2 tablespoons rice vinegar

2 tablespoons ketchup

¼ cup soy sauce

2 tablespoons sugar

¼ cup chicken broth, low-sodium preferred

½ teaspoon sesame oil

1 tablespoon hoisin sauce

1 tablespoon cornstarch

⅓ cup roasted peanuts

6 cups cooked long-grain white rice, for serving

DIRECTIONS

1. In a wok or large skillet, heat the olive oil over high heat. Add the chicken and cook for 5–6 minutes, until almost no pink remains

2. Add the red, yellow, and orange bell peppers; green onions; garlic; and ginger. Cook for 5 minutes.

3. Add the snow peas and red pepper flakes and cook for an additional minute.

4. In a medium bowl, combine the rice vinegar, ketchup, soy sauce, sugar, chicken broth, sesame oil, hoisin sauce, and cornstarch, then add to the wok with the peanuts and cook for 1 minute until the sauce thickens.

5. Serve over hot rice.

Chicken and Waffle Sliders

Yield: 10 sliders | Prep Time: 5 minutes | Cook Time: 3 minutes

When you have leftover Honey Barbecue Chicken Poppers (page 17), make sure to come back to this recipe. It's great to have in your back pocket when your kids invite friends over and you want to give them a quick treat. Since it uses ready-made chicken nuggets and mini toaster waffles, the hardest thing you will have to do is whip up the spicy maple drizzle. Just be sure to make a few extra because you'll want some too!

INGREDIENTS

½ cup good-quality maple syrup

3 tablespoons sriracha or other hot sauce, plus more as needed

½ (10.9-ounce) package Eggo Minis waffles

10 Honey Barbecue Chicken Poppers (page 17)

DIRECTIONS

1. In a small saucepan, heat the maple syrup. Add the sriracha sauce and stir well. Simmer for 2 minutes and then remove from the heat. Taste and adjust the spice level, if necessary.

2. Toast the mini waffles according to the package directions.

3. Reheat the Honey Barbecue Chicken Poppers if necessary.

4. To serve, separate the mini waffles and place a Popper on top of ten of them. Drizzle generously with the spicy syrup. Top with the remaining waffle to create mini sandwiches.

Pesto Chicken with Zucchini Noodles

Yield: Serves 2 | Prep Time: 10 minutes plus 30 minutes marinade time | Cook Time: 8–10 minutes

Zucchini noodles (or "zoodles") are all the rage. Seriously, it seems like if you haven't spiralized a vegetable yet, you're behind the times. Don't worry if you've never tried it before. Use this recipe as an opportunity to see what all the fuss is about.

INGREDIENTS

2 boneless, skinless chicken breasts

1 tablespoon pesto, plus more as needed

½ teaspoon kosher salt, plus more as needed

¼ teaspoon freshly ground black pepper, plus more as needed

2 zucchini, trimmed and spiralized (see notes)

6–8 sun-dried tomatoes in oil, drained and chopped

Shredded Italian-blend cheese (optional)

DIRECTIONS

1. In a medium bowl, combine the chicken, pesto, salt, and pepper. Toss to coat.

2. Cover and let marinate in the refrigerator for 30 minutes or longer.

3. Grill or sauté the chicken over medium heat for 4–5 minutes per side until fully cooked. Place on a cutting board and let rest for 5 minutes. Slice the chicken.

4. In a large skillet sprayed with cooking spray, add the zucchini noodles with salt and pepper to taste. Heat for 1–2 minutes over medium-high heat.

5. Place the zucchini noodles in a bowl or on a platter.

6. Top the noodles with the sliced chicken, sun-dried tomatoes, more pesto, and shredded Italian cheese, if using. Serve.

NOTES

To spiralize: Trim the ends of the zucchini so they're flat. Straight pieces work best, so if your zucchini is crooked, cut it at the bend so you have straighter pieces to work with. Insert the zucchini into the spiralizer and turn the handle to create your noodles.

Caesar Chicken and Kale

Yield: Serves 4 │ Prep Time: 5 minutes │ Cook Time: 15 minutes

Kale is one of those superfoods that it seems like we always hear so much about. It's jam-packed with vitamins A, K, and C, among others, making this dish a must-have for any health-conscious meal plan. This is a dinner recipe you can feel really good about eating!

INGREDIENTS

2 tablespoons olive oil

4 boneless, skinless chicken breasts

Kosher salt and freshly ground black pepper

3 tablespoons store-bought Caesar dressing, plus more as needed

1 tablespoon chopped fresh parsley

6 cups chopped kale

¼ cup shredded Parmesan cheese

Juice of ½ lemon

¼ cup croutons

Lemon wheels, for garnish

DIRECTIONS

1. In a large skillet, heat the olive oil over medium-high heat. Season the chicken generously with salt and pepper. Add the chicken to the pan and cook for 5 minutes on each side until cooked through and golden brown on both sides. Transfer the chicken to a plate and cover with aluminum foil.

2. To the same pan, set over medium-low heat, add the Caesar dressing and chopped parsley, stirring to warm it through and to scrape up any flavorful bits from the bottom of the pan. Add the kale and season generously with salt and pepper. Stir and cook for 2–3 minutes until the kale is wilted. Add up to ⅛ cup water to the pan to help the kale wilt, if needed. Remove from the heat and return the chicken to the pan. Sprinkle with Parmesan cheese, croutons, and lemon juice. Garnish with lemon wheels and serve.

Chicken Potpie Biscuit Sliders

Yield: Serves 6–8 | Prep Time: 20 minutes | Cook Time: 15 minutes

It's Grandma's go-to chicken dinner . . . with a twist! This handheld version of chicken potpie is a real crowd-pleaser among kids since they don't have to use a fork and knife. You'll just need to make sure you have some wet wipes on hand to clean up afterward!

INGREDIENTS

1 (16.3-ounce) can refrigerated biscuits

⅓ cup unsalted butter

1 small onion, diced

2 garlic cloves, minced

1 celery stalk, diced

1 carrot, diced

⅓ cup all-purpose flour

¾ cup chicken broth

½ cup white wine

¾ cup half-and-half

1 teaspoon Dijon mustard

1 teaspoon fresh thyme, minced

½ teaspoon kosher salt

¼ teaspoon freshly ground black pepper

2 boneless, skinless chicken breasts, cooked and diced or shredded (about 2 cups)

¾ cup frozen peas

DIRECTIONS

1. Bake the biscuits according to the package instructions.

2. Meanwhile, in a large skillet, melt the butter. Add the onion, garlic, celery, and carrot. Cook for 4–5 minutes, until the vegetables are softened.

3. Sprinkle the flour over the cooked vegetables, then whisk in the chicken broth, white wine, and half-and-half.

4. Cook until thick, 1–2 minutes. Stir in the Dijon mustard, thyme, salt, and pepper.

5. Add the chicken and peas and stir together to warm, about 3 minutes. Remove from the heat.

6. To serve, slice the biscuits in half and scoop ¼ cup of the chicken mixture onto each biscuit. Put the other half of each biscuit on top and serve.

NOTES

To cook the chicken, place the breasts on a baking sheet and bake at 350°F for 30 minutes.

Smothered Chicken 'n' Gravy

Yield: Serves 4 | Prep Time: 10 minutes | Cook Time: 40 minutes

The southern United States can boast some of the best recipes around. They're full of comfort-food ingredients cooked from the heart. The chopped onion and celery add a crunchy pop of texture that brings the whole dish together.

INGREDIENTS

½ cup all-purpose flour

1 teaspoon kosher salt

¼ teaspoon smoked paprika or cayenne pepper

¼ teaspoon freshly ground black pepper

2 pounds boneless, skinless chicken breasts

4 tablespoons (½ stick) unsalted butter

½ cup chopped onion

½ cup chopped celery

3 cups chicken broth, low-sodium preferred

½ cup heavy cream (optional)

Chopped and whole parsley, for garnish

Mashed potatoes, for serving

DIRECTIONS

1. In a large zip-top bag, combine the flour, salt, paprika, and pepper and shake to mix. Add the chicken and close the top; use your hands to thoroughly coat the chicken with the flour mixture. Transfer the chicken pieces onto a plate. Reserve the remaining flour mixture.

2. In a large, deep skillet, melt the butter over medium-high heat. Add the chicken and cook for 3–4 minutes per side, until lightly browned. Moderate the heat if necessary to be sure the butter does not brown or burn. The chicken may not be completely cooked; it will continue to cook in a later step.

3. Transfer the chicken to a plate and set aside. Add the onion and celery to the pan and sauté, stirring, until the onion turns translucent, about 2 minutes. Add the remaining dredging flour to the pan and cook, stirring, until all the flour has been absorbed, about 1 minute. Add the chicken broth and return the chicken to the pan. Cover and cook over medium heat for 20–30 minutes, until fragrant and heated through. Taste and adjust the seasonings if necessary. Stir in the cream (if using) and cook for an additional minute.

4. Garnish with the parsley. Serve with mashed potatoes.

Lemon Butter Chicken

Yield: Serves 4–6 | Prep Time: 15 minutes | Cook Time: 20–25 minutes

My favorite part about this recipe has to be the sauce. It has a creamy texture with a hint of fresh lemon that gives me a warm and cozy feeling every time I taste it.

INGREDIENTS

2 tablespoons olive oil

1 (8-ounce) container sliced cremini mushrooms

2 tablespoons unsalted butter

5 boneless, skinless chicken breasts

1 tablespoon fresh lemon juice

1 cup dry white wine

1 cup heavy cream

Kosher salt and freshly ground black pepper

Lemon wheels and fresh rosemary, for garnish

DIRECTIONS

1. Pound the chicken into ½-inch thickness. In a large skillet, heat the olive oil over medium heat. Add in the mushrooms and sauté for 2–5 minutes until tender and lighlty browned. Add the butter and cook until melted. Add the chicken breasts and sear them on both sides until lightly browned, about 5 minutes on each side.

2. Add the lemon juice, wine, and cream. Simmer for 10 minutes. Season with salt and pepper.

3. Add the lemon wheels and rosemary and serve from the skillet with the sauce.

Chicken Parmesan

Yield: Serves 2 | Prep Time: 20 minutes | Cook Time: 10 minutes

You can never really go wrong when you've got an Italian favorite like Chicken Parmesan on the menu. Serve this by itself or cook some spaghetti to serve alongside. You can even set up a few candles and turn on soft music to make it a date night!

INGREDIENTS

2 boneless, skinless chicken breasts

⅛ teaspoon kosher salt

⅛ teaspoon freshly ground black pepper

½ cup all-purpose flour

1 large egg, beaten

¾ cup panko bread crumbs

½ teaspoon dried Italian seasoning

3 tablespoons grated Parmesan cheese

2 tablespoons olive oil

Small loaf ciabatta bread, halved, or 2 large ciabatta rolls

2 slices mozzarella cheese

⅓ cup marinara sauce, heated

DIRECTIONS

1. Place the chicken breasts between two sheets of plastic wrap and pound them to a ½-inch thickness. Sprinkle with salt and pepper.

2. Place the flour and egg in separate bowls.

3. In another small bowl, combine the panko, Italian seasoning, and Parmesan cheese.

4. Dip the chicken in the flour first, then in the egg, and lastly in the bread crumb mixture.

5. In a large skillet, heat the olive oil over medium heat. Add the chicken and cook until golden, 4–5 minutes per side.

6. Cut the ciabatta in half horizontally. Place each chicken breast on the bread, top with marinara sauce and add a slice of mozzarella. Serve warm.

Chicken Broccoli Alfredo

Yield: Serves 4–6 | Prep Time: 15 minutes | Cook Time: 20 minutes

I love using cavatappi in this recipe because the curves in the pasta soak up all the flavors from the soup and cheese. If you want try something different, substitute shells or penne pasta.

INGREDIENTS

½ (16-ounce) box cavatappi pasta

1 cup fresh or frozen broccoli florets

2 tablespoons unsalted butter

1 pound boneless, skinless chicken breasts, cut into cubes

1 (10.5-ounce) can cream of mushroom soup

½ cup whole milk

½ cup grated Parmesan cheese, plus more for serving

¼ teaspoon freshly ground black pepper

DIRECTIONS

1. Bring a large pot of water to a boil. Add the cavatappi pasta and cook until al dente. Add the broccoli for the last 4 minutes of the cooking time. Drain and set aside.

2. In a large, deep skillet, melt the butter over medium heat. Add the chicken and cook until browned, stirring often, about 5 minutes.

3. Add the cream of mushroom soup, milk, Parmesan cheese, pepper, and the pasta mixture and heat through. Serve with additional Parmesan cheese.

6

Oven-Baked

Some of my favorite memories are of walking into a toasty kitchen and smelling the aroma of a homemade baked chicken dinner, wafting through the air. I want to share those kinds of memories with my family, too, which is why oven-baked chicken dinners are absolute mainstays.

One-Pan Chicken and Potatoes

Yield: Serves 4 | Prep Time: 5 minutes | Cook Time: 35–40 minutes

I could eat these potatoes off the pan all day long, even cold! The buttery flavor makes Yukon Gold potatoes so comforting. I usually end up buying a couple of extra potatoes to satisfy my own snacking habit.

INGREDIENTS

4 boneless, skinless chicken breasts

6–8 Yukon Gold potatoes, quartered or halved

2 cups baby carrots

1 red onion, quartered

10–15 garlic cloves, peeled and left whole

Kosher salt and freshly ground black pepper

1 tablespoon chopped fresh rosemary

1 tablespoon chopped fresh thyme

2 tablespoons chopped fresh parsley

2 tablespoons olive oil

DIRECTIONS

1. Preheat the oven to 375°F. Line a baking sheet with aluminum foil.

2. Arrange the chicken, potatoes, carrots, onion, and garlic cloves on the baking sheet in a single, even layer. Sprinkle the chicken and vegetables with salt and pepper and the rosemary, thyme, and parsley. Drizzle everything with the olive oil. Gently toss with your fingers and rearrange in a single layer.

3. Bake for 35–40 minutes until the chicken is cooked through and the vegetables are tender.

4. Transfer to a serving dish and serve immediately.

Creamy Chicken Crescent Roll-Ups

Yield: 8 rolls | Prep Time: 10 minutes | Cook Time: 25 minutes

Refrigerated crescent rolls are a genius kitchen shortcut that I use often when I'm pressed for time. You can fill them up with just about anything, throw them in the oven, and serve up a buttery, flaky dream. This easy dinner recipe is just one example of crescent roll cooking done right.

INGREDIENTS

1 medium boneless, skinless chicken breast, cooked and cubed (about 1 cup)

4 ounces cream cheese, softened

1 (10.5-ounce) can cream of chicken soup

1 tablespoon canned chopped pimento, drained

1 (8-ounce) can refrigerated crescent rolls

2 tablespoons unsalted butter, melted

½ cup panko bread crumbs

1 tablespoon grated Parmesan cheese

¼ teaspoon dried Italian seasoning

½ cup shredded mozzarella or white cheddar cheese

2 tablespoons whole milk

DIRECTIONS

1. Preheat the oven to 350°F. Line a baking sheet with parchment paper.

2. In a medium bowl, combine the chicken, cream cheese, ½ cup of the cream of chicken soup, and half of the pimento, stirring until smooth and well mixed.

3. On a work surface, unroll the rolls and separate into 8 pieces. Place a heaping tablespoon of the chicken mixture on the wide end of each, fold the corners in toward the filling, and roll up. Place on the prepared baking sheet and brush them with melted butter.

4. Combine the panko, Parmesan cheese, and Italian seasoning and sprinkle each roll generously with the mixture. Bake for 25 minutes until the rolls are browned and baked through.

5. Meanwhile, place the remaining soup and pimento into a small saucepan. Add the mozzarella cheese and stir over low heat until the cheese melts, adding milk as necessary to create a sauce-like consistency.

6. Serve the hot rolls with the sauce on the side.

NOTES

To cook the chicken, place the breast on a baking sheet and bake at 350°F for 30 minutes.

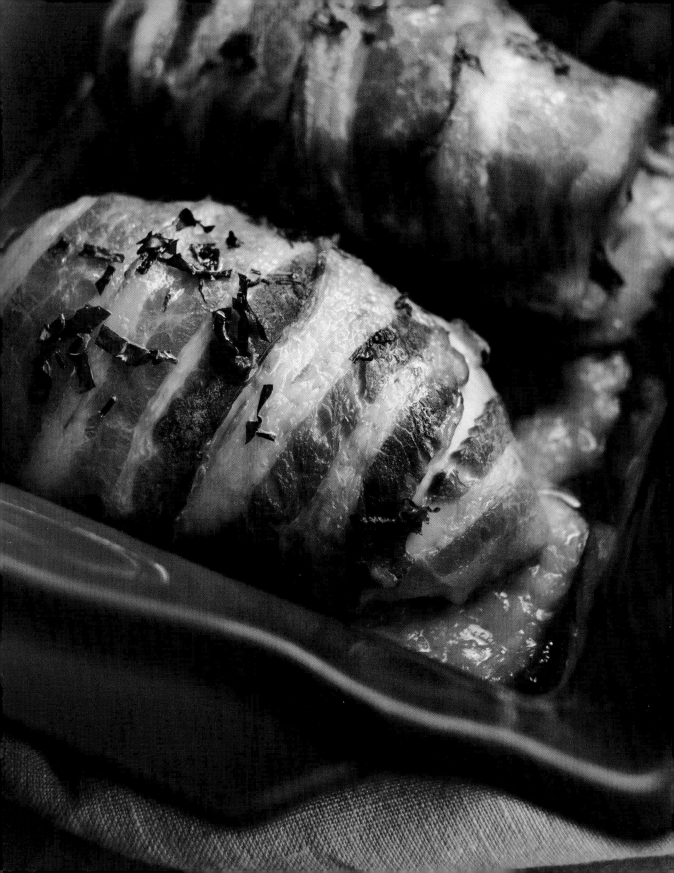

Bacon-Wrapped Stuffed Chicken

Yield: Serves 4 | Prep Time: 20 minutes | Cook Time: 45–50 minutes

When making these stuffed chicken breasts, briefly freezing the cheese sticks beforehand will prevent them from melting and spilling out before the chicken is cooked.

INGREDIENTS

4 ounces Swiss cheese, cut from a block into long sticks

2 tablespoons unsalted butter

½ cup finely chopped onion

4 ounces button mushrooms, stemmed and sliced

2 tablespoons chopped fresh parsley

¼ teaspoon grated nutmeg

4 boneless, skinless chicken breasts

½ teaspoon kosher salt

¼ teaspoon freshly ground black pepper

6 bacon slices

DIRECTIONS

1. Preheat the oven to 350°F. Spray a 7 × 10-inch baking dish with cooking spray.

2. Place the cheese sticks in the freezer while prepping the remaining ingredients, about 20 minutes.

3. In a medium skillet, melt the butter over medium-high heat. Add the onion and cook for 2–4 minutes, stirring, until translucent. Add the mushrooms, half the parsley, and the nutmeg and cook, stirring, until the mushrooms begin to brown and the juices evaporate, about 3 minutes.

4. While the onions and mushrooms cook, cut the chicken horizontally and open like a book, placing it between two sheets of plastic wrap and pounding it if necessary to a ½-inch thickness. Sprinkle with salt and pepper.

5. When the vegetables are cooked, lay one stick of cheese on each pounded chicken breast and top with one-quarter of the mushroom mixture. Tuck in the sides, then roll the chicken into a neat roll with the seam side down. Wrap each chicken breast completely with a slice of bacon, tucking the ends securely underneath—if the chicken breasts are large, you may need 1–2 additional bacon slices to wrap them entirely.

6. Place the chicken seam-side down in the baking dish, sprinkle with the remaining parsley, and bake for 45 minutes, or until the chicken is cooked through. Serve.

Beer Can Chicken

Yield: Serves 4 | Prep Time: 20 minutes plus 20 minutes resting | Cook Time: 60–75 minutes

When I first heard about this recipe, I had two thoughts: 1) *This is one of the most ridiculous recipes I've ever seen.* 2) *When can I try it out?* It looks a little flashy, so make sure you try it out sometime when you have an audience to please. They won't be able to resist how it's moist and juicy on the inside, and crisp and flavorful on the outside.

INGREDIENTS

1 (12-ounce) can of beer

2 garlic cloves, peeled and left whole

1 (4–5-pound) whole chicken, neck and giblets removed from the cavity

3 tablespoons packed light brown sugar

2 teaspoons kosher salt

2 teaspoons ground cumin

1 teaspoon freshly ground black pepper

1 teaspoon Mexican-style chili powder

1 teaspoon garlic powder

½ teaspoon onion powder

3 tablespoons unsalted butter, softened

2 limes, thinly sliced

3 tablespoons olive oil

DIRECTIONS

1. Preheat the oven to 425°F.

2. Open the can of beer and pour one-quarter of the can into a large oven-safe skillet or baking dish. Drop the garlic cloves into the can and set it in the center of the skillet.

3. Rinse the chicken well. Pat it dry with paper towels.

4. In a small bowl, stir together the brown sugar, salt, cumin, pepper, chili powder, garlic powder, and onion powder.

5. In another small bowl, mix the butter and one-third of the spice mix together until smooth. Using your thumbs, carefully lift the skin of the chicken and rub the butter under the skin. Gently slide lime slices under the skin all around the chicken.

6. Place the chicken on top of the beer can, sliding the can into the chicken cavity as far as it will go, keeping the chicken in an upright position.

7. Rub the entire chicken well with olive oil. Press the remaining spice mixture into the skin all over.

8. Roast the chicken for about 1 hour. The chicken is done when the thermometer reads an internal temperature of 165°F, the skin is crispy, and the flesh is firm. Remove the pan from the oven and let the chicken rest for 20 minutes. Using kitchen tongs, gently remove the can from the chicken. Slice and serve.

Roasted Garlic Chicken Pizza

Yield: Serves 6–8 | Prep Time: 20 minutes | Cook Time: 20 minutes

I love making pizza at home. It's a fun activity to do with friends or family, and the garlicky chicken plus asparagus make this pizza a complete meal, vegetables included!

INGREDIENTS

1 (13.8-ounce) can refrigerated pizza dough

All-purpose flour, for dusting

1 cup marinara sauce

1 cup shredded mozzarella cheese

2 boneless, skinless chicken breasts, cooked and shredded (see note)

4 garlic cloves, minced

1 pound asparagus, blanched, cooled, and cut into 2-inch pieces

1 cup grated Parmesan cheese

2 tablespoons olive oil

DIRECTIONS

1. Preheat the oven to 400°F. Line a pizza tray with parchment paper.

2. Roll out the pizza dough on a floured surface. Place on the pizza tray.

3. Top with the marinara sauce, mozzarella cheese, chicken, garlic, asparagus, and Parmesan cheese. Drizzle with olive oil.

4. Bake for 20 minutes until the crust is golden brown and the cheese is bubbling.

5. Remove from the oven, allow to cool slightly, and serve.

NOTES

To cook the chicken, place the breasts on a baking sheet and bake at 350°F for 30 minutes.

Baked Firecracker Chicken

Yield: Serves 6 | Prep Time: 20 minutes | Cook Time: 25 minutes

If you're looking for a spice-filled challenge, then you've come to the right recipe. This chicken dish is hot, hot, hot! Dare yourself to use a hot sauce that's spicier than you'd normally try. You can always cool down with extra white rice for serving!

INGREDIENTS

1 cup packed light brown sugar

½ cup bottled hot sauce

1 tablespoon apple cider vinegar

1 teaspoon finely minced garlic

½ teaspoon celery salt

¼ teaspoon red pepper flakes, plus more as needed

2 pounds boneless, skinless chicken thighs

1 tablespoon vegetable oil

Cooked white rice, for serving

Parsley, for garnish

DIRECTIONS

1. Preheat the oven to 400°F. Line a baking sheet with aluminum foil or a silicone baking mat.

2. In a small saucepan, combine the brown sugar, hot sauce, apple cider vinegar, garlic, celery salt, and red pepper flakes. Bring to a boil over medium heat, then reduce the heat to maintain a simmer and cook, stirring occasionally, for 15 minutes.

3. While the sauce is cooking, lay the chicken thighs in a single layer, smooth-side down, on the baking sheet. Brush with the vegetable oil and bake for 5 minutes. Turn the chicken smooth-side up and brush liberally with a third of the sauce. Bake for 5 minutes, then brush again with another third of the sauce. Bake for 15 minutes until the chicken is cooked through and beginning to char along the edges.

4. Serve over cooked white rice, garnish with parsley, and pass around the remaining sauce at the table.

Almond-Crusted Chicken

Yield: Serves 4 | Prep Time: 15 minutes | Cook Time: 25–30 minutes

When I go to the local farmers' market, I'm always trying to figure out what protein I should pair with the interesting new veggie I just picked up. This delightful dish often comes to mind. It's so simple that it's easy to pair off with just about anything, and the nutty flavor makes it worth savoring every time!

INGREDIENTS

1 cup sliced almonds

1 cup panko bread crumbs

1 tablespoon fresh rosemary leaves

3 tablespoons unsalted butter

¾ cup all-purpose flour

1 teaspoon kosher salt

½ teaspoon freshly ground black pepper

2 large eggs

4 boneless, skinless chicken breasts (about 1½ pounds)

DIRECTIONS

1. Preheat the oven to 400°F. Line a baking sheet with aluminum foil or parchment paper.

2. In a food processor, combine the almonds, panko, and rosemary leaves and pulse to coarse crumbs. In a medium skillet, melt the butter over medium-high heat. Add the almond mixture and toast until golden brown and fragrant, about 2 minutes. Transfer to a pie plate or shallow bowl. In another pie plate or shallow bowl, combine the flour, salt, and pepper. In a small bowl, beat the eggs with 1 tablespoon of water.

3. Dip each chicken breast into the flour until lightly coated, then into the egg mixture, and finally into the crumb mixture until well coated. Place the chicken on the prepared baking sheet and bake for 20–25 minutes until golden brown and cooked through. Serve.

Chicken Thighs with Mushroom Sauce

Yield: Serves 4 | Prep Time: 10 minutes | Cook Time: 35 minutes

Mushrooms are comforting, and they're an easy way to dress up chicken, making this dish a weeknight favorite in my house. Chicken thighs bathed in the luscious mushroom sauce also make ideal leftovers, thinly sliced on sandwiches.

INGREDIENTS

8 boneless, skinless chicken thighs (about 4 pounds)

1 teaspoon salt

⅛ teaspoon freshly ground black pepper

2 tablespoons chopped fresh rosemary, plus sprigs for garnish

2 tablespoons chopped fresh thyme, plus sprigs for garnish

2 tablespoons olive oil

8 ounces fresh button mushrooms, halved

1 tablespoon all-purpose flour

1 cup chicken broth, low-sodium preferred

½ cup white wine

2 tablespoons Dijon mustard

1 tablespoon chopped fresh flat-leaf parsley, plus whole leaves for garnish

DIRECTIONS

1. Preheat the oven to 400°F.

2. Season the chicken with salt, pepper, 1 tablespoon of the rosemary, and 1 tablespoon of the thyme.

3. In a 12-inch cast-iron skillet or very large oven-safe skillet, heat the olive oil over medium heat. Add the chicken, skin-side down, and cook for 5–7 minutes until browned on one side. Turn the chicken pieces over, transfer the pan to the oven, and bake for 15–20 minutes.

4. Remove the chicken from the skillet and set aside.

5. Add the mushrooms to skillet and set over medium-high heat; cook, stirring occasionally, for 4 minutes. Add the flour to the skillet, stirring the mushrooms to coat. Stir in the chicken broth, wine, and mustard. Cook, stirring, until thickened and bubbling, 2–3 minutes. Remove the skillet from the heat and add the remaining rosemary, and thyme, and the parsley.

6. Serve the mushroom sauce over chicken. Garnish with parsley, thyme, and rosemary.

Chicken Pastry Turnovers

Yield: Serves 8 | Prep Time: 20 minutes | Cook Time: 20–25 minutes

These turnovers look innocent enough upon first glance, but once your guests pierce their forks through the buttery, flaky crust, they'll be pleasantly surprised to see the chicken and veggie mixture tumbling out. It's like being greeted with a warm hug at the end of a long day.

INGREDIENTS

5½ tablespoons unsalted butter

1 small onion, diced

2 garlic cloves, minced

1 celery stalk, diced

1 carrot, diced

⅓ cup all-purpose flour

¾ cup chicken broth, low-sodium preferred

½ cup white wine

¾ cup half-and-half

1 teaspoon Dijon mustard

1 teaspoon fresh thyme, minced, plus more for garnish

½ teaspoon kosher salt

¼ teaspoon freshly ground black pepper

2 boneless, skinless chicken breasts, cooked and diced or shredded (about 2 cups)

¾ cup frozen peas, thawed

1 (14.1-ounce) package refrigerated pie crusts

1 egg white

1 tablespoon whole milk

DIRECTIONS

1. Preheat the oven to 400°F. Line a baking sheet with parchment paper.

2. In a large skillet, melt the butter. Add the onion, garlic, celery, and carrot. Cook for 4–5 minutes, until the vegetables are softened. Sprinkle the flour over the vegetables, then whisk in the chicken broth, white wine, and half-and-half.

3. Cook until thick, 1–2 minutes. Stir in the Dijon mustard, thyme, salt, and pepper. Add the chicken and peas. Remove from the heat.

4. Unroll the pie crusts and, using a rolling pin, thin them out slightly. Using a bowl that is 5 inches across, cut out 4 circles of dough from each pie crust.

5. Spoon as much filling as you can in the center of each circle of dough.

6. In a small bowl, combine the egg white and milk. Use a pastry brush to wet the edges of the dough with the egg mixture. Fold the dough in half to create a semicircle, pressing to seal the edges. Crimp around the edges with a fork.

7. Place on the baking sheet and brush the tops of the turnovers with the remaining egg mixture. Bake for 15–18 minutes until golden brown. Garnish with thyme and serve.

NOTES

To cook the chicken, place the breasts on a baking sheet and bake at 350°F for 30 minutes.

Easy Baked Chicken Nuggets

Yield: 24 nuggets | Prep Time: 10 minutes | Cook Time: 20 minutes

There's no need to buy chicken nuggets from the frozen food aisle or the fast food drive-through when it's this easy to make them right at home! If you'd like, experiment with different dipping sauces to please everyone at the table.

INGREDIENTS

1 pound boneless, skinless chicken breasts or chicken tenders

¼ cup all-purpose flour

1 teaspoon onion powder

½ teaspoon kosher salt

1 teaspoon paprika

¼ teaspoon cayenne pepper (optional; see note)

¼ cup vegetable oil

Honey mustard or ranch dressing, for dipping

DIRECTIONS

1. Preheat the oven to 450°F. Line a baking sheet with aluminum foil, parchment paper, or a silicone mat.

2. If using whole chicken breasts, cut them crosswise into 6 strips, or approximately ½ × 2-inch pieces. (Tenders may be used without further cutting.) In a large zip-top bag, combine the flour, onion powder, salt, paprika, and cayenne pepper and drop the chicken into the bag. Seal the bag and shake well to completely coat the chicken with the flour mixture.

3. Arrange the coated chicken pieces 1 inch apart on the prepared baking sheet. Use a pastry brush to coat each piece of chicken with the vegetable oil. Bake for 15 minutes, turn over, and bake for an additional 5 minutes.

4. Serve with honey mustard or ranch dressing for dipping.

NOTES

If you are making these for children, you may wish to omit the cayenne pepper; or increase the amount if you have a family who enjoys spicy dishes.

Roasted Chicken

Yield: Serves 4–6 | Prep Time: 5 minutes plus 20 minutes resting | Cook Time: 1 hour 15 minutes

Simple roasted chicken doesn't get the love and attention it deserves. While the bird itself may seem intimidating, it takes minimal effort. And if you add a few herbs and veggies, you'll have a fancy meal worth bragging about!

INGREDIENTS

1 (4- to 5-pound) whole chicken, neck and giblets removed from the cavity

1 tablespoon olive oil

2 tablespoons kosher salt

Freshly ground black pepper

1 lemon, sliced

Fresh herbs, such as parsley, rosemary, or thyme (optional)

1 pound multicolored potatoes, cut in half

1 onion, coarsely chopped

4 garlic cloves

DIRECTIONS

1. Arrange a rack in the middle of the oven and preheat the oven to 425°F.

2. Rinse the chicken well. Place it on a work surface or cutting board and pat it dry with paper towels. Cut off and discard any extra fat hanging around the body cavity.

3. Drizzle the olive oil on the chicken and rub it all over the skin. Season generously inside and out with salt and pepper. Place the lemon and the herbs (if using) inside the cavity. Place the chicken breast-side up in a large frying pan or cast-iron skillet.

4. Surround the chicken with the potatoes, onion, and garlic.

5. Roast the chicken for 15 minutes. Reduce the oven temperature to 375°F and roast until the juices run clear and a thermometer inserted into the inner thigh (but not touching the bone) registers 165°F, an additional 50 minutes to 1 hour.

6. Remove the chicken from the oven and place on a cutting board. Let it rest for 15–20 minutes before carving.

7. Serve over the potatoes, onion, and garlic.

7

Casseroles

From church suppers to book clubs to neighborhood potlucks, there's almost never an occasion where a casserole isn't appropriate. Savor these dishes yourself or make them for friends and family to enjoy!

Butter Chicken Cracker Casserole

Yield: Serves 4–6 | Prep Time: 15 minutes | Cook Time: 25–30 minutes

I love using crackers as a breading with recipes because it gives them an extra bit of buttery flavor (and a satisfying crunch to boot!). This shortcut recipe is simple enough to make on a busy Monday night, and you'll still have leftovers to enjoy throughout the week.

INGREDIENTS

3 medium boneless, skinless chicken breasts, cooked and shredded (about 3 cups)

1 (10.5-ounce) can cream of chicken soup

1 cup sour cream

1 cup frozen peas, thawed

6 ounces Ritz crackers, crushed into fine crumbs

4 tablespoons (½ stick) unsalted butter, melted

½ teaspoon paprika

DIRECTIONS

1. Preheat the oven to 350°F. Coat a 9 × 13-inch baking dish with cooking spray.

2. In a large bowl, combine the shredded chicken, cream of chicken soup, sour cream, and peas. Stir well. Pour into the prepared baking dish.

3. In a small bowl, combine the crushed crackers, butter, and paprika until the mixture resembles wet sand. Spoon evenly on top of the casserole and bake for 25–30 minutes until the filling is bubbling and the top is lightly browned. Slice and serve.

NOTES

To cook the chicken, place the breasts on a baking sheet and bake at 350°F for 30 minutes.

Skinny Chicken Enchilada

Yield: Serves 6 | Prep Time: 20 minutes | Cook Time: 20–25 minutes

Enchiladas are often made on the stovetop or in a toaster oven, but this one gets the oven-baked treatment. It's much easier to cut out the exact portion that you want instead of getting stuck with a whole tortilla you might not be able to finish.

INGREDIENTS

12 (6-inch) corn tortillas

2 (16-ounce) jars salsa verde

2 medium boneless, skinless chicken breasts, cooked and shredded (about 2 cups)

1 small white onion, finely diced

1 cup shredded Mexican-blend cheese

½ cup chopped fresh cilantro, plus whole leaves for garnish

1 jalapeño, seeded and finely diced

Cotija cheese, for garnish

DIRECTIONS

1. Preheat the oven to 400°F. Lightly coat a 9 × 13-inch baking dish with cooking spray.

2. Wet paper towels and wrap two layers around the corn tortillas. Microwave for 45 seconds until soft and pliable.

3. Pour 1 jar of the salsa over the bottom of the prepared baking dish. Fill each tortilla with about 3 tablespoons of chicken, 1 tablespoon of onion, and 1 tablespoon of the Mexican-blend cheese, and sprinkle with cilantro and jalapeño. Roll the tortilla and place seam-side down in the baking dish. Repeat with the remaining tortillas. Pour the second jar of salsa over the top of the tortillas. Top with the remaining Mexican-blend cheese.

4. Bake for 20–25 minutes until bubbling. Top with cotija cheese and cilantro leaves.

5. Let cool for 5 minutes before serving.

NOTES

To cook the chicken, place the breasts on a baking sheet and bake at 350°F for 30 minutes.

Chicken Potpie Casserole

Yield: Serves 6–8 | Prep Time: 15 minutes | Cook Time: 30 minutes

This shortcut version of a traditional chicken potpie is simple enough to throw together whenever the mood strikes you. Plus, it has all the veggies baked right in, so you don't have to worry about sides.

INGREDIENTS

1 (16-ounce) bag frozen mixed stir-fry vegetables, thawed

3 boneless, skinless chicken breasts, cooked and chopped (about 3 cups)

1 (10.5-ounce) can cream of chicken soup

1 cup biscuit baking mix

½ cup whole milk

1 large egg

DIRECTIONS

1. Preheat the oven to 400°F.

2. In an ungreased 8-inch round or square baking dish, mix together the vegetables, chicken, and cream of chicken soup.

3. In a small bowl, mix the baking mix, milk, and egg with a fork until blended. Pour into the baking dish.

4. Bake for 30 minutes or until golden brown. Serve.

NOTES

To cook the chicken, place the breasts on a baking sheet and bake at 350°F for 30 minutes.

Creamy Chicken and Kale Casserole

Yield: Serves 8–10 | Prep Time: 30 minutes | Cook Time: 30 minutes

Chicken and kale are a match made in heaven. You have the health benefits of the superfood kale along with the comfort of creamy chicken and multiple Italian cheeses.

INGREDIENTS

1 (13.25-ounce) box rigatoni or penne pasta

1 tablespoon unsalted butter

2 tablespoons olive oil

1 large onion, finely diced

1 garlic clove, minced

1½ pounds kale, stems and ribs removed, leaves torn or cut into bite-size pieces

3 medium boneless, skinless chicken breasts, cooked and chopped or shredded (about 3 cups)

24 ounces part-skim ricotta cheese

8 ounces mascarpone cheese

1 cup shredded Italian-blend cheese

1 cup grated Parmesan cheese

1 tablespoon lemon zest

½ cup fresh parsley, finely chopped

1 cup panko bread crumbs

1 tablespoon fresh thyme, finely chopped

DIRECTIONS

1. Preheat the oven to 350°F. Lightly coat a 9 × 13-inch baking dish with cooking spray.

2. Bring a large pot of water to a boil. Add the rigatoni and cook until al dente. Drain and return the pasta to the pot.

3. In a large skillet, melt the butter with 1 tablespoon of the olive oil. Add the onions and garlic and cook until tender, 3–5 minutes. Add the kale, cover, and cook until the kale is wilted and tender, 3–5 minutes. Add to the pot with the pasta.

4. Mix in the chicken, ricotta cheese, mascarpone cheese, Italian-blend cheese, ¾ cup of the Parmesan cheese, the lemon zest, and the parsley. Transfer the mixture to the casserole dish.

5. In a small bowl, combine the panko, the remaining ¼ cup Parmesan cheese, and the thyme. Sprinkle the mixture over the casserole. Drizzle with the remaining 1 tablespoon olive oil.

6. Bake for 30 minutes until golden brown and hot. Slice and serve.

NOTES

To cook the chicken, place the breasts on a baking sheet and bake at 350°F for 30 minutes.

Golden Mushroom and Chicken Casserole

Yield: Serves 8 | Prep Time: 30 minutes | Cook Time: 1 hour

This dish reminds me of a casserole my aunt used to make for me whenever I'd come visit around the holidays. I remember loving the combination of mushroom and chicken and feeling so content after dinner that I'd fall asleep on the couch while we were watching TV.

INGREDIENTS

4–5 large boneless, skinless chicken breasts, cut into 1-inch-thick strips

½ teaspoon kosher salt

¼ teaspoon freshly ground black pepper

1 cup plus 3 tablespoons all-purpose flour

6 tablespoons olive oil

1 pound fresh mushrooms, sliced

2 large shallots, finely minced

3 garlic cloves, minced

3 tablespoons unsalted butter

1 cup chicken broth, low-sodium preferred

½ cup marsala or white wine

1 tablespoon fresh lemon juice

1 cup heavy cream

1 tablespoon fresh rosemary, finely minced, plus more for garnish

DIRECTIONS

1. Preheat the oven to 350°F. Lightly coat a 9 × 13-inch baking dish with cooking spray.

2. Season the chicken with salt and pepper. Put 1 cup of the flour in a shallow bowl. Dredge the chicken in the flour.

3. In a large skillet, heat 3 tablespoons of the olive oil. Add the chicken and cook until golden brown, 10–12 minutes. Do not crowd the pan; work in batches if necessary.

4. Transfer the chicken to the baking dish.

5. Wipe out the pan and add the remaining 3 tablespoons olive oil, the mushrooms, and the shallots. Cook until tender, about 3 minutes, then add the garlic and cook for 1–2 minutes more, until fragrant. Pour over the mixture over the chicken.

6. In the same skillet, melt the butter. Whisk in the remaining 3 tablespoons flour and cook for 1–2 minutes, until slightly thickened.

7. Add the chicken broth, wine, and lemon juice. Whisk, then add the heavy cream and bring to a simmer. Add the rosemary and season with salt and pepper if needed.

8. Pour the sauce over the chicken and mushrooms. Cover the dish with aluminum foil and bake for 45 minutes.

9. Garnish with rosemary and serve.

Greek Yogurt Chicken and Rice Casserole

Yield: Serves 6 | Prep Time: 20 minutes | Cook Time: 35 minutes

The unique tangy flavor of this casserole tricks your guests into thinking you labored in the kitchen all day long. The secret to getting this lovely tanginess without any trouble at all is the Greek yogurt. Use leftover chicken on a weekday, and you'll have a new meal in 35 minutes.

INGREDIENTS

4 tablespoons olive oil

8 ounces cremini mushrooms, sliced

1 onion, chopped

2 tablespoons all-purpose flour

2½ cups chicken broth, low-sodium preferred

4 medium boneless, skinless chicken breasts, cooked and shredded (about 4 cups)

2 cups cooked white rice

½ cup Greek yogurt

Kosher salt and freshly ground black pepper

1 cup shredded cheddar cheese blend

½ cup fresh parsley, for garnish

DIRECTIONS

1. Preheat the oven to 375°F.

2. In a large skillet, heat 2 tablespoons of the olive oil over medium heat. Add the mushrooms and onion. Cook, stirring, until the mushrooms are tender and browned, 10 minutes. Add the remaining 2 tablespoons oil and the flour. Stir to combine and cook for 1 minute.

3. Add the chicken broth and bring to a boil, whisking constantly. Add the chicken and rice and return to a simmer. Stir in the Greek yogurt; season with salt and pepper. Transfer the mixture to an 8-inch square baking dish. Top with the cheddar.

4. Bake until the cheese is melted and the mixture is warm throughout, 15–20 minutes.

5. Serve warm, garnished with parsley.

NOTES

To cook the chicken, place the breasts on a baking sheet and bake at 350°F for 30 minutes.

King Ranch BBQ Chicken Casserole

Yield: Serves 10 | Prep Time: 20 minutes | Cook Time: 50 minutes

One of my best friends spends a lot of time on the King Ranch, a big, beautiful place in Texas. This meal reminds me of my time with her in Texas, where we spent mornings running around the ranch and evenings toasting marshmallows and eating BBQ chicken.

INGREDIENTS

3 tablespoons olive oil

1 tablespoon paprika

1 tablespoon chili powder

2 teaspoons ground cumin

1 teaspoon kosher salt

2 pounds boneless, skinless chicken breasts, cut into 1-inch cubes

1 cup diced green bell pepper

1 cup diced onion

1 jalapeño pepper, seeded and finely diced

1 garlic clove, finely minced

1 (10.5-ounce) can cream of chicken soup

1 (10.75-ounce) can cheese soup

1 (10-ounce) can RoTel tomatoes, undrained

16 ounces shredded Mexican-blend cheese

10 (6-inch) corn tortillas, cut into quarters

3 cups crushed tortilla chips

DIRECTIONS

1. Preheat the oven to 350°F. Lightly coat a 9 × 13-inch baking dish with cooking spray.

2. In a large bowl, combine 2 tablespoons of the olive oil, the paprika, chili powder, cumin, and salt. Add the cubed chicken and toss to coat.

3. In a large deep skillet, add the remaining 1 tablespoon oil, the bell pepper, onion, and jalapeño and cook over medium-high heat, stirring frequently, for about 10 minutes, or until the vegetables are softened and aromatic.

4. Add the chicken and garlic and cook, stirring, for another 10 minutes. The chicken will be browned and mostly cooked through.

5. In a large bowl, combine the cream of chicken soup, cheese soup, and the tomatoes. Stir well.

6. Set aside 1 cup of the cheese. Make layers in the casserole dish as follows: half the cooked chicken mixture, half the cheese, half the tortilla pieces, and half the soup mixture. Repeat.

7. Bake, uncovered, for 20 minutes. Remove from the oven and add the crushed corn tortilla chips, top with the remaining 1 cup shredded cheese and bake for 10 minutes more, until the cheese is melted and beginning to brown. Slice and serve.

Layered Chicken and Spaghetti Casserole

Yield: Serves 6 | Prep Time: 20 minutes | Cook Time: 15 minutes

It's easy to just give up on spaghetti, relegating it to the confines of "spaghetti and meatballs" territory. But when you combine the comforting presence of spaghetti with the reliable casserole format, you get a unique and memorable dish.

INGREDIENTS

6 boneless, skinless chicken breasts, cooked and shredded

1 pound spaghetti

1 (24-ounce) jar marinara sauce

1 (10.5-ounce) can cream of chicken soup

1 onion, chopped

Parsley, for garnish

DIRECTIONS

1. Preheat the oven to 400°F.

2. Bring a large pot of water to a boil. Add the spaghetti and cook until al dente. Drain.

3. In a large bowl, combine the pasta with all the remaining ingredients except the parsley.

4. Pour the mixture into a 9 × 13-inch baking dish and cover with aluminum foil.

5. Cook for 15 minutes until bubbling and warm all the way through.

6. Garnish with parsley and serve.

NOTES

To cook the chicken, place the breasts on a baking sheet and bake at 350°F for 30 minutes.

One-Pot Chicken Cordon Bleu

Yield: Serves 8–10 | Prep Time: 25 minutes | Cook Time: 50 minutes

When you want to feel fancy, make this casserole. My husband and I sometimes like to have "Date Night In," where we get all dressed up to have a fancy meal in the kitchen. Compliments all go to the chef, of course.

INGREDIENTS

4 boneless, skinless chicken breasts, cooked and shredded

½ pound ham steak, cut into bite-size cubes

4 ounces sliced Jarlsberg cheese

½ cup (1 stick) unsalted butter

¼ cup all-purpose flour

3 cups half-and-half

2 tablespoons fresh lemon juice

1 tablespoon Dijon mustard

¾ teaspoon kosher salt

½ teaspoon smoked paprika

¼ teaspoon freshly ground white pepper

1½ cups panko bread crumbs

½ teaspoon sea salt

1½ teaspoons herbes de Provence

Sprigs of fresh thyme, for garnish

DIRECTIONS

1. Preheat the oven to 350°F. Lightly coat a 9 × 13-inch baking dish with cooking spray.

2. Place the chicken in the baking dish. Layer the ham over the chicken. Layer the Jarlsberg over the chicken and ham.

3. In a large saucepan, melt half of the butter over medium heat. Whisk in the flour to form a roux, being careful not to burn the mixture. When the roux is smooth, slowly whisk in the half-and-half. Switch to a wooden spoon and stir until the sauce is thick, about 5 minutes.

4. Stir in the lemon juice, mustard, kosher salt, paprika, and white pepper.

5. Bring the sauce to a low simmer, then remove from the heat.

6. Pour the sauce over the casserole, making sure it covers all the corners.

7. For the topping, melt the remaining butter in a medium microwaveable bowl. Stir in the panko, sea salt, and herbes de Provence. Sprinkle the mixture over the casserole.

8. Bake for 45 minutes until the top is golden and the casserole is hot.

9. Garnish with thyme and serve warm.

NOTES

To cook the chicken, place the breasts on a baking sheet and bake at 350°F for 30 minutes.

"Don't Peek" Chicken

Yield: Serves 4–5 | Prep Time: 10 minutes | Cook Time: 1 hour 15 minutes

When you're really hungry, sometimes it's hard not to take a quick peek at a dish before it's done. This is one of those dinners that's going to test your patience. Keep it covered right up until it's done cooking to make sure the heat stays sealed in, and I promise you won't be disappointed.

INGREDIENTS

1 cup uncooked long-grain white rice

1 (10.5-ounce) can cream of mushroom soup

1 (10.5-ounce) can cream of chicken soup

1 (1-ounce) package onion soup mix

1 (10.75-ounce) can chicken broth, low-sodium preferred

1 garlic clove, crushed

1 teaspoon chopped fresh parsley

1 teaspoon Worcestershire sauce

4–5 boneless, skinless chicken breasts

1 teaspoon paprika

Sprigs of fresh sage, for garnish

DIRECTIONS

1. Preheat the oven to 350°F. Lightly coat a 9 × 13-inch baking dish with cooking spray.

2. In a large bowl, combine the rice, cream of mushroom soup, cream of chicken soup, onion soup mix, chicken broth, garlic, parsley, and Worcestershire sauce.

3. Pour the mixture into the baking dish. Nestle the chicken into the mixture.

4. Sprinkle the paprika over the chicken.

5. Cover with aluminum foil. Bake for 1 hour 15 minutes. DO NOT PEEK during baking! Garnish with sage and serve.

Buffalo Chicken Casserole

Yield: Serves 8 | Prep Time: 1 hour | Cook Time: 1 hour

Need something to bring over for watching the big championship game? This hot 'n' ready casserole has just enough kick to keep you on your toes until the clock runs out.

INGREDIENTS

8 boneless, skinless chicken thighs

Kosher salt and freshly ground black pepper

6 bacon slices, chopped

3 jalapeños, seeded and chopped, plus slices for garnish

1½ (8-ounce) packages cream cheese, softened

½ cup mayonnaise

½ cup hot sauce

8 ounces shredded cheddar cheese

4 ounces shredded mozzarella cheese

Chopped fresh cilantro, for garnish

DIRECTIONS

1. Preheat the oven to 400°F. Line a baking sheet with aluminum foil.

2. Season the chicken thighs well with salt and pepper and place on the baking sheet. Bake for 40 minutes until cooked through.

3. Meanwhile, in a large skillet, cook the bacon over medium heat for 10 minutes. Add the jalapeños and cook until the bacon is crisp. Without draining the pan, add the cream cheese, mayonnaise, and hot sauce to the skillet. Mix together well and taste for seasoning. The hot sauce can be quite salty, so avoid adding salt until tasting.

4. Coat a 9 x 13-inch baking dish with cooking spray. Remove the chicken from the oven and add to the casserole dish in an even layer. Top with the cream cheese mixture. Sprinkle an even layer of cheddar and mozzarella cheese over the top, mixing them together as you sprinkle.

5. Bake for 10–15 minutes. Switch the oven to broil and broil for 5 minutes to lightly brown the cheese on top.

6. Garnish with chopped cilantro and sliced jalapeños and serve.

Make-Ahead Chicken

Yield: Serves 6 | Prep Time: 25 minutes plus overnight chilling | Cook Time: 1 hour 5 minutes

When you're running low on time, sometimes you need to prep ahead to get yourself out the door. This Make-Ahead Chicken can be chilled overnight, so all you need to do the next day is pop it in the oven.

INGREDIENTS

2 large boneless, skinless chicken breasts

½ teaspoon kosher salt

¼ teaspoon freshly ground black pepper

1 bay leaf

1 cup shredded cheddar cheese

1 (10.5-ounce) can cream of celery soup

1 teaspoon Dijon mustard

2 cups frozen mixed vegetables, thawed

2 cups medium shells pasta (about 5 ounces), uncooked

1 (3.4-ounce) sleeve Ritz crackers, crumbled

2 tablespoons unsalted butter, melted

Sprigs of fresh parsley, for garnish

DIRECTIONS

1. Place the chicken in a small saucepan and cover with 2½ cups of water. Add the salt, pepper, and bay leaf and simmer over medium heat for 20 minutes. Remove the chicken and strain and measure the liquids—you should have 2 cups; add water if necessary to make that amount.

2. Cut the chicken into ½-inch cubes and place in a large bowl with half the cheddar, the cream of celery soup, and mustard. Add the reserved broth, mixed vegetables, and pasta shells, and stir until well mixed.

3. Coat an 8-inch square baking dish with cooking spray and pour the mixture into it, adding the remaining cheddar on top. Cover tightly and chill overnight.

4. Preheat the oven to 350°F.

5. Uncover the dish and bake for 30 minutes. Sprinkle with the crackers, then pour the butter over all. Bake for another 15 minutes until the filling is bubbling and the topping is lightly browned. Garnish with parsley and serve.

Wicked Cheesy Chicken and Pasta

Yield: Serves 4 | Prep Time: 15 minutes | Cook Time: 45 minutes

This wicked good dinner has all the makings of a new classic. With pasta, chicken, Alfredo sauce, and cheese, it'd be hard to find anyone who'd turn this down.

INGREDIENTS

8 ounces cavatappi pasta, uncooked

4 boneless, skinless chicken breasts

Kosher salt and freshly ground black pepper

Garlic powder

Red pepper flakes

1 tablespoon olive oil

1 (15-ounce) jar Poblano Alfredo sauce, or 1 (15-ounce) jar regular Alfredo sauce combined with 1 (4-ounce) can green chiles, drained

1 cup shredded Italian-blend cheese

¼ cup grated Parmesan cheese

DIRECTIONS

1. Preheat the oven to 350°F. Lightly coat a 9 × 13-inch baking dish with cooking spray.

2. Bring a large pot of water to a boil. Add the cavatappi and cook until al dente. Drain and set aside.

3. Season the chicken with salt, pepper, garlic powder, and red pepper flakes.

4. In a large skillet, heat the olive oil over medium heat. Add the chicken and brown for 3 minutes on each side.

5. Add the pasta to the baking dish and top with the chicken.

6. Pour the Alfredo sauce over all and mix to combine.

7. Add the cheeses to the top of the casserole and bake for 30 minutes. Serve.

Chicken and Swiss Casserole

Yield: Serves 4 | Prep Time: 10 minutes | Cook Time: 30–35 minutes

This is the kind of "welcome home" casserole your family is going to love you for making. Whether your spouse is away on a business trip or the kids are just coming back from camp, nothing says "I missed you" like a homemade meal.

INGREDIENTS

2 slices white bread

4 medium boneless, skinless chicken breasts, cooked and chopped (about 4 cups)

⅔ cup mayonnaise

½ cup thinly sliced celery

½ cup whole milk

½ teaspoon kosher salt

¼ teaspoon freshly ground black pepper

½ cup chopped green onion, including some of the green tops

6 ounces Swiss cheese, shredded

Sprigs of fresh sage, for garnish

DIRECTIONS

1. Preheat the oven to 350°F. Coat an 8-inch square baking dish with cooking spray.

2. Cut the bread into ½-inch cubes and toast on a baking sheet for 2–3 minutes until golden brown.

3. In a large bowl, combine the bread, chicken, mayonnaise, celery, milk, salt, and pepper and toss to mix. Add all but 2 tablespoons each of the green onion and cheese to the bowl, and stir. Pour into the prepared baking dish and top with the remaining green onion and cheese.

4. Bake for 30–35 minutes until the casserole is warmed through and the cheese is melted. Garnish with sage and serve.

NOTES

To cook the chicken, place the breasts on a baking sheet and bake at 350°F for 30 minutes.

Chicken Gloria Casserole

Yield: Serves 6 | Prep Time: 20 minutes | Cook Time: 45 minutes

If you're looking for a showstopper dish you can make when you really need to impress company, then this is just the casserole you need. The inclusion of both a protein and a side dish all in one meal allows you to cut down on your planning while still presenting a dish that's super filling.

INGREDIENTS

Chicken

½ cup all-purpose flour

½ teaspoon kosher salt

¼ teaspoon freshly ground black pepper

6 boneless, skinless chicken breasts

2 tablespoons olive oil

2 tablespoons unsalted butter

1 cup white button mushrooms, sliced

¼ cup chopped fresh parsley

1 teaspoon fresh thyme leaves, or ½ teaspoon dried thyme

½ cup sherry

½ cup chicken broth, low-sodium preferred

1 cup whole milk or half-and-half

6 slices Muenster cheese

Sprigs of fresh thyme, for garnish

Rice

6 servings wild and brown rice mix

1½ cups chicken broth, low-sodium preferred, or as rice package directs

¼ cup chopped fresh parsley

DIRECTIONS

1. *For the chicken:* Preheat the oven to 350°F. Coat a 9 × 13-inch baking dish with cooking spray.

2. In a pie plate or shallow bowl, combine the flour, salt, and pepper. Dredge the chicken breasts in the mixture, patting with your fingers to coat them evenly. Reserve the flour mixture.

3. In a large heavy-bottom skillet, heat the oil over medium-high heat. Sauté the chicken until light golden brown for about 3 minutes on each side. Transfer the chicken to the baking dish in a single layer.

4. In the same skillet, melt the butter over medium-high heat and sauté the mushrooms, parsley, and thyme, stirring until the mushrooms are lightly browned, about 4 minutes. Add the reserved flour mixture and cook, stirring constantly, for 2 minutes.

5. Add the sherry and stir until almost evaporated, about 1 minute. Add the broth and milk and reduce the heat to medium. Cook, stirring, until a thick sauce has formed, 3–5 minutes. Pour the sauce over the chicken and lay one slice of Muenster on each piece.

6. Cover the dish with aluminum foil and bake for 30 minutes. Switch the oven to broil. Remove the foil and place the dish under the broiler just until the cheese is browned, about 2 minutes.

7. *For the rice:* While the chicken bakes, prepare the rice with the broth according to the package directions. Stir in the parsley.

8. Serve the rice with the chicken and its sauce. Garnish with thyme.

Chicken, Kale, and Artichoke Bake

Yield: Serves 8 | Prep Time: 15 minutes plus 5 minutes resting time | Cook Time: 40 minutes

Packed full of pasta, chicken, cheese, and veggies, this casserole combines the familiar flavors I love in artichoke dip with ingredients to make a divine main course.

INGREDIENTS

16 ounces rigatoni

1 (15-ounce) jar Alfredo sauce

3 medium boneless, skinless chicken breasts, cooked and shredded (about 3 cups)

1 cup chopped cooked kale

1 (14-ounce) can water-packed quartered artichoke hearts, drained

Kosher salt and freshly ground black pepper

8 ounces mozzarella cheese, shredded

½ cup grated Parmesan cheese

½ teaspoon grated nutmeg

DIRECTIONS

1. Preheat the oven to 400°F.

2. Bring a large pot of water to a boil. Add the rigatoni and cook until al dente. Drain and return the pasta to the pot.

3. Coat a 9 × 13-inch baking dish with cooking spray and set aside.

4. Add the Alfredo sauce, chicken, kale, artichoke hearts, 1 teaspoon salt, and pepper to the pasta. Stir to combine. Season with additional salt and pepper if necessary.

5. Pour half the pasta into the bottom of the baking dish. Top with half the mozzarella cheese and half of the Parmesan cheese. Add the remaining pasta and top with the remaining cheeses and the nutmeg.

6. Bake for 35 minutes. Switch the oven to broil and broil about 5 minutes until the cheese is browned. Let rest for 5 minutes before serving.

NOTES

To cook the chicken, place the breasts on a baking sheet and bake at 350°F for 30 minutes.

Baked Sour Cream Chicken

Yield: Serves 4 | Prep Time: 20 minutes | Cook Time: 1 hour

It's a little unusual to see sour cream being used in this fashion. Usually you see it in recipes for dips! Trust me, though—you'll have a lot of impressed family members when you present this at the dinner table.

INGREDIENTS

1 cup shredded Italian-blend cheese

1 cup sour cream

½ cup mayonnaise

1 cup undiluted cream of chicken soup (about ½ can)

1 teaspoon Dijon mustard

1 tablespoon Worcestershire sauce

2 pounds boneless, skinless chicken tenders

½ cup shredded Parmesan cheese

2 tablespoons chopped fresh parsley, plus extra for garnish

½ teaspoon smoked paprika

Cooked brown rice, for serving

DIRECTIONS

1. Preheat the oven to 350°F. Coat an 8-inch square baking dish with cooking spray.

2. In a large bowl, combine 1 cup of the Italian-blend cheese, the sour cream, mayonnaise, cream of chicken soup, mustard, and Worcestershire sauce. Add the chicken pieces, tossing to coat the chicken well. Pour into the prepared baking dish, cover tightly with aluminum foil, and bake for 45 minutes, stirring once about halfway through. Remove the foil, sprinkle with the Parmesan cheese, parsley, and paprika and bake, uncovered, for another 15 minutes.

3. Serve with brown rice and garnish with additional parsley.

Chicken Rotini Bubble Up

Yield: Serves 6 | Prep Time: 30 minutes | Cook Time: 1 hour

This dish has a beautifully golden crust. The biscuits on top look like a lattice on a pie or a wicker basket. Not only the perfect comfort food, this recipe is also a showstopper for any potluck.

INGREDIENTS

8 ounces rotini

2 tablespoons unsalted butter

4 carrots, chopped

1 (12-ounce) bag frozen mixed vegetables

Kosher salt

¾ cup all-purpose flour

4½ cups chicken broth, low-sodium preferred

1 cup half-and-half

½ teaspoon dried thyme

3 medium boneless, skinless chicken breasts, cooked and chopped (about 3 cups)

1 (16.3-ounce) can refrigerated biscuits

DIRECTIONS

1. Preheat the oven to 350°F. Coat a 9 × 13-inch baking dish with cooking spray.

2. Bring a large pot of water to a boil. Add the rotini and cook until al dente. Drain and set aside.

3. In a large skillet, melt the butter over medium-high heat. Add the mixed vegetables and 1 teaspoon salt and cook until softened and lightly browned, 5–7 minutes.

4. Stir in the flour and cook, stirring constantly, until lightly browned, about 1 minute. Gradually whisk in 1 cup of the chicken broth and cook until thickened. Slowly whisk in the remaining broth, the half-and-half, and thyme.

5. Add the chicken, vegetable mixture, and pasta and bring to a boil. Reduce the heat to low and simmer for 15 minutes, or until the sauce has thickened. While the chicken mixture is simmering, open the can of biscuits and cut each one into four pieces.

6. Pour the chicken mixture into the prepared baking dish. Place the biscuit pieces all over the top of the dish, completely covering the pasta.

7. Bake for 25 minutes, or until the edges are bubbling and the biscuits are golden brown. Serve.

NOTES

To cook the chicken, place the breasts on a baking sheet and bake at 350°F for 30 minutes.

Doritos Hot Dish

Yield: Serves 6–8 | Prep Time: 35 minutes | Cook Time: 40 minutes

Yes, that's right. We're using Doritos in our dinner. If there's anything that's going to get the kids to run to the table, this is going to be it. I like to use the Nacho Cheese kind in this recipe, but if you want to experiment, try the Cool Ranch!

INGREDIENTS

4 boneless, skinless chicken breasts

Kosher salt and freshly ground black pepper

1 (10-ounce) can RoTel tomatoes, drained

1 (10.5-ounce) can cream of mushroom soup

4 cups shredded cheddar cheese

1 tablespoon taco seasoning

1 (10-ounce) bag Doritos

DIRECTIONS

1. Preheat the oven to 400°F. Line a baking sheet with aluminum foil. Coat a 9 × 13-inch baking dish with cooking spray.

2. Season the chicken with salt and pepper. Place the chicken on the baking sheet and bake for 20 minutes.

3. Remove from the oven and shred the chicken. Reduce the oven temperature to 350°F.

4. In a large bowl, combine the chicken, tomatoes, cream of mushroom soup, 1 cup of the cheddar, and the taco seasoning. Stir well.

5. Cover the bottom of the baking dish with a layer of the Doritos. Top with the chicken mixture and half of the remaining cheddar.

6. Add another layer of Doritos, chicken mixture, and cheddar. Top with the remaining Doritos.

7. Bake for 20 minutes. Serve.

Potato Chip Chicken and Noodle Casserole

Yield: Serves 4–5 | Prep Time: 15–20 minutes plus 5 minutes cooling time | Cook Time: 30 minutes

My favorite thing about this casserole has got to be the texture. The crushed potato chips add a nice crunch while the chicken soup makes it oh-so-creamy.

INGREDIENTS

1 pound boneless, skinless chicken breasts, cooked and cut into chunks

2 celery stalks, chopped

1 tablespoon chopped onion

¼ teaspoon kosher salt

¼ teaspoon freshly ground black pepper

¼ teaspoon sweet paprika

2 cups cooked spaghetti

¼ cup sour cream

1 (10.5-ounce) can cream of chicken soup

1 cup crushed potato chips

Hot sauce, for garnish

DIRECTIONS

1. Preheat the oven to 350°F. Lightly coat an 8-inch square baking dish with cooking spray.

2. In a large bowl, combine the chicken, celery, onion, salt, pepper, paprika, spaghetti, sour cream, and cream of chicken soup and mix well.

3. Pour the mixture into the baking dish. Top with the crushed potato chips.

4. Bake for 30 minutes until golden. Let it cool for 5 minutes before serving. Top with hot sauce.

NOTES

To cook the chicken, place the breasts on a baking sheet and bake at 350°F for 30 minutes.

Chicken and Spinach–Stuffed Shells

Yield: Serves 5–6 | Prep Time: 25–30 minutes | Cook Time: 25 minutes

Stuffed shells may seem a bit too tricky at first, but once you practice on the first two, it's really not that bad. If spooning the mixture into the shells doesn't work, try putting it in a large zip-top bag, cutting off a corner, and piping the mixture through.

INGREDIENTS

1 tablespoon olive oil

9 ounces fresh spinach

2 medium boneless, skinless chicken breasts, cooked and shredded (about 2 cups)

15 ounces ricotta cheese

2¼ cups grated Parmesan cheese

1¼ cups shredded Italian-blend or mozzarella cheese

¼ teaspoon grated nutmeg

½ teaspoon kosher salt

Freshly ground black pepper

1 large egg

1 (12-ounce) box jumbo pasta shells, cooked to al dente

6 tablespoons (¾ stick) unsalted butter

2 cups heavy cream

Fresh basil, chopped or torn, for garnish

DIRECTIONS

1. Preheat the oven to 375°F. Lightly coat a 9 × 13-inch baking dish with cooking spray.

2. In a medium sauté pan, heat the olive oil. Add the spinach and cook just until wilted, 2–3 minutes. Transfer to a cutting board and coarsely chop.

3. In a large bowl, combine the spinach, chicken, ricotta cheese, ¾ cup each of the Parmesan and Italian-blend cheeses, the nutmeg, salt, ¼ teaspoon pepper, and the egg. Mix well.

4. Spoon the filling into 18–20 shells. Set aside.

5. Melt the butter and cream in a medium saucepan over medium heat. Whisk in the remaining 1½ cups Parmesan cheese and simmer, whisking often, until the sauce has thickened and is creamy. Add a few pinches of pepper.

6. Ladle half the sauce into the bottom of the baking dish. Place the filled shells on top of the sauce. Ladle the remaining sauce over the shells and top with the remaining ½ cup Italian-blend cheese.

7. Bake for 20 minutes until the casserole is hot and the cheese is melted. Garnish with fresh basil and serve.

NOTES

To cook the chicken, place the breasts on a baking sheet and bake at 350°F for 30 minutes.

Acknowledgments

When I think of chicken, I think of 13 ladies. Adriana, my best friend and maid of honor, planned an epic trip to the middle of nowhere, Canada. We went glamping. Somehow a beach met a vineyard met the woods and out came Fronterra. There was delicious wine, friendly livestock, warm water, and comfortable cuisine and beds. This was the most spectacular place to spend the weekend celebrating my soon-to-be wedding. I loved being there with ladies who—for four days—showered in lake water, outdoor Canadian water, and never unzipped their makeup bags. Thank you to Sarah, Alice, Emily, Kelly, Mei-Ling, Chrissy, Hazel, Kimrie, Ellen, Erin, Jen, and Kyleigh. No one will ever understand or love chickens the way we do.

Thank you to my incredible culinary and creative team at Prime Publishing. Megan Von Schönhoff and Tom Krawczyk, my amazing photographers. Chris Hammond, Judith Hines, and Marlene Stolfo, my culinary test kitchen geniuses. To word masters and editors Bryn Clark and Jessica Thelander. And to my amazing editor and friend, Kara Rota.

Thank you to Stuart Hochwert and the entire Prime Publishing team for your enthusiasm and support. Thank you to Will Schwalbe, Erica Martriano, Justine Sha, Jaclyn Waggner, and the entire staff at St. Martin's Griffin for helping this book come to life. This book was a team effort, filled with collaboration and creativity that reached no limits.

Index

About the Author

After receiving her masters in culinary arts at Auguste Escoffier in Avignon, Addie Gundry stayed in France to learn from Christian Etienne at his three-Michelin-star restaurant. Upon leaving France, she spent the next several years working with restaurant groups. She worked in the kitchen for Daniel Boulud and moved coast to coast with Thomas Keller building a career in management, restaurant openings, and brand development. She later joined Martha Stewart Living Omnimedia, where she worked with the editorial team as well as in marketing and sales. While living in New York, Addie completed her bachelor's degree in organizational behavior. Upon leaving New York, Addie joined gravitytank, an innovation consultancy in Chicago. As a culinary designer at gravitytank, Addie designed new food products for companies, large and small. She created edible prototypes for clients and research participants to taste and experience, some of which you may see in stores today. In 2015 she debuted on the Food Network, where she competed on *Cutthroat Kitchen*, and won! In the summer of 2017 she competed on the thirteenth season of *Food Network Star*.

Addie is the executive producer for RecipeLion. She oversees and creates culinary content for multiple web platforms and communities, leads video strategy, and oversees the production of in-print books. She is passionate about taking easy recipes and making them elegant without making them complicated. From fine dining to entertaining, to innovation and test kitchens, her experience with food makes these recipes unique and delicious.

Addie and her husband live in Lake Forest, Illinois, with their baby boy and happy puppy, Paisley. She is actively involved with youth culinary programs in the Chicagoland area, serving on the board of a bakery and catering company that employs at-risk youth. She is also a healthy-food teacher for first-graders in a low-income school district and, aside from eating and entertaining with friends and family, she loves encouraging kids to be creative in the kitchen!